CONTENTS

ISBN: 0-87441-412-1

PUBLISHED BY BEHRMAN HOUSE, INC.

Millburn, NJ

STUDY QUESTIONS BY DR. ROBERT L. PLATZNER

COVER/BOOK DESIGN BY ROBERT J. O'DELL

MANUFACTURED IN THE UNITED STATES OF AMERICA

Library of Congress Cataloging-in-Publication Data

Main entry under title:

Midrash: Rabbinic lore.

    1. Midrash—Translations into English. 2. Aggada—

Translations into English. I. Gersh, Harry.

BM512.M48   1985   296.1'4205   85-15662

INTRODUCTION

ALL SERIOUS BOOKS RAISE MORE QUESTIONS THAN THEY answer. Certainly the book taken most seriously by Jews, the Bible, raised a multitude of questions. Even those parts of the book that seemed easy to understand raised questions of who and how and why. But this was no ordinary book to be made clearer by rewriting and adding and rearranging. The Scriptures came to the Jews directly from God. And a book from God could not be changed by mortals. So the deeper meanings hidden behind the simplest stories and messages had to be found by searching the book itself.

Over the centuries, each rereading raised new explanations, interpretations, and answers to the various questions. The Hebrew word for "search" or "investigation" is *midrash*. The explanatory interpretations found through this method are called *midrashim*.

The Scriptures include law, history, poetry, prophecy, philosophy, and much more. Each of these different branches of Scripture required a different kind of explanation, of midrash. So there is *midrash halakhah*, an investigation or explanation of law, and *midrash aggadah*, stories that teach.

Midrash halakhah mainly covers the legal portions of Torah, the Book of Leviticus, for example. This kind of midrash seeks to define the laws of Torah, to uncover principles of Torah law, and to bring out, not new laws, but laws hidden within the basic law. Midrash halakhah also finds scriptural support for traditional customs and practices already accepted by the people.

Midrash aggadah deals mainly with the story parts of the Scriptures. It seeks new meanings hidden in these stories and highlights the ethical and moral messages in the narratives. For example, the *Haggadah*, the book we read at the Passover *seder*, is midrash aggadah. In this aggadah we get not only the story of the Exodus, taken from Torah, but midrashic explanations of what this story means. (*Haggadah* and *aggadah* are the same words. They both come from the Hebrew word *heged*, "to recount" or "to teach.")

Nowadays, Jews tend to use the two words, midrash and aggadah, to mean the same thing: stories that illustrate or teach a religious lesson. These stories can be entertaining to read and hear, but they were not written or told solely to entertain. They are lessons put into a form, enjoyable to hear and easy to understand. For most people it is easier to listen to a fable that teaches a moral lesson than to listen to the legal language of the law. Fables are far more likely to be remembered than dry legal language.

Midrash probably began during the time of the prophets—the 8th century B.C.E. Both Isaiah [29:21] and Amos [5:10] tell of prophets who "reproved at the gates" of the city. This would be a natural place for prophets and storytellers, since this was where markets were held and people gathered. The prophets often gave their messages through parables, stories that taught a lesson. When they "reproved" the people, they didn't just say you must not do this, you must do that. They told parables of what happened when people broke the law and of the great rewards to those who lived by the Torah.

That aggadic storytelling was a common teaching method is also suggested in other verses of Scripture. Nehemiah reports how the Torah was explained to the Jews on their return to Jerusalem from the Babylonian exile in the 5th century B.C.E.:

| And they read in the book, in the Law of God, distinctly; and they gave the sense, | and caused them [the people] to understand the reading.   NEHEMIAH 8:8 |

According to the Talmud the Levites "gave the sense" of the biblical narrative by using midrashim to teach the people the real meaning of Torah.

The midrashim told by the Levites in Nehemiah's day probably have been lost to us. Most of the midrashim we know were developed and told during a thousand-year period beginning well before the destruction of the Second Temple (70 C.E.). However, those early midrashim were not written down until many centuries later.

Few classical midrashim were created after 1000 C.E., but many stories that can be included among aggadot and midrashim were created long after. In fact, they are still being created.

NEED FOR MIDRASH

Most midrashim were produced during two very different periods: one, a period of wars and persecutions; the other, a period of relative peace and great intellectual growth. The period of wars included these events: Rome took control of Judah in 63 B.C.E., ending a century of Jewish independence. In 70 C.E., the Temple, center of Jewish religious life, was destroyed. In 135 C.E., the last Jewish state—until the founding of Israel 1,800 years later—was destroyed. Two hundred years later, even the right to live in an organized community was denied to the Jews of the land of Israel.

The period of peace included the centuries during which the Talmud was created in Babylon. These were the early centuries of the Diaspora, a time when Jews had to learn to live under foreign rulers and in foreign lands. They were assailed on all sides by religions and nations more powerful than the Jews. They were surrounded by seemingly more powerful gods, more successful cultures. The law that had guided Jewish life for centuries now had to be interpreted to make life possible under totally new conditions.

The powerful nations and religions that now surrounded the Jews boasted of great heroes who did marvelous things for their people. It was a time when many Jews were beset by doubts; it was a time when they needed to be reminded of their own heroes. They needed to be reminded of the times when God opened the seas for them and armies fell before the hosts of the Lord. They needed to be reminded that their law was The Law.

However, the Scriptures do not feature heroes—at least, not the god-like, totally powerful heroes of the surrounding peoples and cultures. The Book of the Jews does not tell of mortals like gods; it talks of people who are human, with all the faults of humans. None of the Jewish heroes were born miraculously; none were descended from gods. Nor were there any perfect human beings or saints among the Jews. In Scripture, even the greatest of Jewish heroes were ordinary men and women.

When the Jews, in moments of misery and in times of doubt, yearned for superheroes, their preachers gave them superheroes. In the midrashim Jews were even bigger, smarter, and more powerful than the Greek, Roman, Persian heroes. The seeds of the stories were in Scripture; the Rabbis caused the seeds to flower into midrashim.

BIBLICAL SUPERHEROES

For example, every Jew knew from Scripture that King Solomon was a wise and great ruler. The tellers of aggadot made Solomon the wisest and the mightiest of rulers. The Greek Achilles, the Roman Caesar, the Babylonian Marduk were no match for the aggadist's Solomon. However, since Solomon was a Jewish scriptural hero, he had to be human, to have human faults. Even as the storytellers told of Solomon's marvelous deeds, they had to show his arrogance, his pride, his deviousness. He was punished for these faults in the very same aggadot that told us of his greatness.

There is a story, for example, of how Solomon split and formed the stones out of which the Temple was built. According to Torah [DEUTERONOMY 27:5], the Temple's stones could not be split with iron tools. Solomon had to find another way to work the stone. He had to get hold of the *shamir*, the worm (some say the stone) that can split rock [TOSEPHTA 15:1]. According to the midrash, Solomon had a magic ring, which gave him power over demons; he could force the evil creatures to do good rather than evil. He planned to use this magic power to find the shamir. But because Solomon had broken the commandment that prohibits a king from "multiplying" his wives, horses, and gold, Solomon lost his magic ring. He could not find the worm (or stone) that splits rock. The midrash further tells how Solomon outwitted Asmodeus, the chief demon, and how Solomon eventually obtained the *shamir*.

Moses was another favorite character of the aggadists. In story after story he was presented as the greatest and kindest of human beings, not only to other people but to all God's creatures. One midrash tells how, while Moses was caring for his father in-law's sheep, a lamb became tired following the flock. All that day Moses carried the lamb on his shoulders. To give the midrash a practical lesson, the story goes on to say that Moses always pastured the sheep in open country, far from the property of others, so that the sheep would not intrude on someone else's grazing land.

The midrashim had another purpose, as important as providing heroes for the Jews. They allowed the Jews a degree of freedom of speech, not permitted by their foreign overlords. The Jews were not allowed to criticize their conquerers or speak against their governors. So they told stories—aggadot—about Jacob and Esau. Every Jew knew that Jacob represented Israel and Esau represented Rome. Sometimes the storytellers used colors; red always stood for Rome. Even a child knew that Edom was Israel's ancient enemy. Edom was descended from Esau and Esau was redheaded. Consequently, persecutors of the Jews appeared in stories as Esau, Edom, and red.

Often a preacher in synagogue could not speak out directly against persecutions under a Roman general or a Christian king, without danger of torture and death. Then the preacher might tell a story about how a fox outwitted a lion, or how fish cannot escape the fisherman by jumping onto dry land. (*See page 23.*)

Midrashim were used to teach about God and man, to explain the need to obey the laws of God, and to give hope to the Jews in troubled times. Midrash aggadah was a form of art, a kind of theater. Sometimes the story itself was the main thing, but usually its purpose was education in the principles of Judaism.

EARLY MIDRASHIM

Many stories and interpretations that make up midrash were first told during a *d'rashah*, the sermon that explains the Torah portion read during that synagogue service. For centuries before the Talmudic period, Jews gathered three mornings a week to read a portion of the Torah. They gathered together on Mondays, Thursdays, and Shabbat to read successive parts of the Book. Mondays and Thursdays were market days, with little time for more than a short service. But on Shabbat, on holidays, and on days of celebration, such as a wedding day, a scholar would be invited to give his interpretation of the Torah portion. This was the d'rashah. Scholars and rabbis who specialized in these after-service lectures were called *darshanim*, the ones who gave the d'rashah.

A d'rashah had to be both scholarly and simple. It had to be scholarly enough to satisfy the learned ones in the congregation, to make them think that the *darshan* was a learned man. And the d'rashah had to be simple enough so that ordinary folk could say: it was a difficult portion, but the darshan made it clear. For scholars the darshan included tricky combinations of verses from Scripture, new derivations of words, perhaps a new interpretation. For simpler folk, the non-scholars, the d'rashah included stories that explained the portion and made its inner meaning clear.

One caution was necessary: aggadot could teach, but they could not make law. Aggadot were not legal decisions. The Talmud warned:

> No halakhah can be derived from aggadah.
> PEAH 17A (JERUSALEM TALMUD)

So long as he kept this warning in mind, the darshan could let his imagination roam free.

As in all folk tales, aggadot include animals who speak a human language and people who talk with animals. Solomon was said to understand the language of the trees and clouds, of the beasts and birds. The Baal Shem Tov, founder of Hasidism in the 18th century, was said to talk to the creatures of the forest. Rabbi Meir, pupil of Akiba (2nd century), was said to have told over 300 fables or parables with foxes as the main characters. This is one:

> The Angel of Death was casting one of each species of animal into the sea. When it was the fox's turn, the Angel of Death went looking for a fox. He found the fox wailing on the shore of a river. "Why are you crying?" the Angel of Death asked the fox. "Because my brother has been thrown into the water and has drowned." The Angel of Death looked into the water and there was a fox, exactly like the one on shore. Thinking he had already killed one of the species fox, Death passed on. And the fox laughed and laughed because he had fooled Death. It was only the fox's reflection in the water that Death had seen.

COLLECTING AND PUBLISHING MIDRASHIM

Collections of halakhic midrashim, explanations of the law, were made even before the Mishnah was written down. The *Mekhilta*, meaning "measure" or "rule," is a collection of midrash halakhah based on the book of Exodus, and was compiled in the second century. *Sifra*, from the Aramaic word for "book," is a collection of midrashim on the book of Leviticus. *Sifre*, the plural of sifra, is a collection of halakhic midrashim based on Numbers and Deuteronomy. Both *Sifra* and *Sifre* were also collected during the second century.

Collections of midrash aggadah began appearing about the 5th century. The most important is the *Midrash Rabbah*, the "Great Midrash." These books include aggadot illustrating stories from all five Books of Moses and the five *megillot*: Esther, Ruth, Song of Songs, Ecclesiastes, Lamentations. From this period also comes another famous collection of midrashim aggadot, *Pesikta de Rab Kahana*. These stories elaborate and explain the portions of the Torah read on holidays and special Sabbaths.

These works were part of the first great period of collecting and editing midrashim. The second great period was post-Talmudic, from about 640 to 1000 C.E. During these centuries the Moslem Middle East was the center of the world and of Jewish learning. The major collection of midrashim in this period was made by Tankhuma ben Abba, a famous Palestinian aggadist. His collection is called *Tankhuma Yelammedenu* from the opening words of most of the stories: "Yelammedenu Rabbenu" ("let our master instruct us").

The making of these anthologies did not stop; collections called *Yalkhutim* appeared in the eleventh and twelfth centuries. The largest of these collections is the *Yalkhut Shimoni*, edited by someone known simply as Simon the Preacher. And the work goes on. In our own century, Martin Buber compiled anthologies of midrashim told by and about the great Hasidic rabbis. The great Yiddish storytellers, I.L. Peretz and Sholem Aleichem, wrote stories that fulfill all the requirements of midrashim.

Through midrash halakhah and midrash aggadah, Jews learned the meaning of the Law and its limits. They learned that their sufferings were not in vain and that there was hope for the world and for them. As when an aggadist told this story:

A king married and gave his bride a *ketubah*, a marriage contract. In the contract, the king promised that in the years to come his queen would receive great treasures of gold and jewels and palaces. Then the king left on a long journey. He was away for many, many years, so long that his people said he was never coming back.

The queen remained faithful to her vow, and the queen's friends began to mock her. "How long are you going to wait?" they taunted the bride. "The king will never return. Get yourself another husband while you are still young and beautiful." But the queen would go into her house and read the marriage contract and comfort herself.

After many years, the king did return. He said to his wife: "I marvel that you waited for me so long." She answered: "My lord, I would have lost hope long ago, taken the advice of our friends, but for our ketubah. When I had doubts, I would read our marriage contract and be strengthened."

So it is with this world. The nations of the world mock Israel and say: "How long will you sacrifice yourself for your King, giving up your lives for Him? Give Him up and come over to us and to our gods." Israel replies by going into its houses, its synagogues, and reading the Torah, the Covenant, that God gave to Israel.□

STUDY QUESTIONS

1 What does the word *midrash* actually mean? What is the basic purpose of a midrashic story?

2 When the Rabbis spoke of the Bible as something that came "directly from God," what did they mean?

3 How would a modern Bible scholar attempt to unlock the secrets or answer the questions raised by the Bible?

4 What is the difference between *midrash halakhah* and *midrash aggadah*?

5 How is the Passover *Haggadah* connected to the writing of midrashim?

6 When did Jews first attempt to compose midrashim? Which books of the Bible, so far as we know, became the subjects of midrashic commentaries during the Talmudic period?

7 What is a *d'rashah*? How would a midrashic tale naturally grow out of a d'rashah? Do we have darshanim (or their modern counterparts) living today?

8 Why was there a tendency towards hero worship in the early midrashim? Can you find any evidence of an inclination towards hero worship in modern Jewish thought?

9 In the midrashic tale of the king and his bride what does the ketuba represent? In your own words, restate the meaning of this aggadic parable.

FOR DISCUSSION

Create an aggadic tale of your own that is an elaboration of some biblical narrative.

ושפיכות דמים דכתיב עז זו דא דאמרן גילוי עריות
ושפיכות דמים דתניא ר' אומר °כי כאשר‌זניים
יקום איש על רעהו ורצחו נפש בן הדבר הזה
וכי מה ענין רוצח אצל נערה המאורסה °הרי
זה בא ללמד ונמצא למד מקיש רוצח לנערה
המאורסה מה נערה המאורסה ניתן להצילה
בנפשו °אף רוצח ניתן להצילו בנפשו ונערה
המאורסה מרוצח °מה רוצח יהרג ואל יעבור
אף נערה המאורסה תהרג ואל תעבור
ושפיכות דמים גופיה מנלן סברא הוא °כי
ההוא דאתא לקמיה דרבא א"ל מרי דוראי
אמר לי זיל קטליה לפלני' ואי לא קטלינא לך
א"ל ליקטלוך ולא תיקטול מאי חזית דדמא
דידך סמק טפי דילמא דמא דההוא גברא
סמק טפי מר בר רב אשי אשכחיה לרבינא
דשייף לה לברתיה בגוהרקי דערלה אמר ליה
אימור דאמר רבנן בשעת הסכנה שלא
בשעת הסכנה מי אמר א"ל האי אישתא
צמירתא נמי כשעת הסכנה דמיא איבא דאמרי
א"ל °מי דרך הנאה קא עבידנא איתמר
הנאה הבאה לו לאדם בעל כרחו אביי אמר
מותרת ורבא אמר אסור אפשר וקא מיכוין
לא אפשר וקמיכוין כולי עלמא לא פליגי
דאסור לא אפשר ולא מיכוין כולי עלמא לא
פליגי דשרי °כי פליני דאפשר ולא מיכוין
ואליבא דר' יהודה דאמר °דבר שאין מתכוין
אסור כולי עלמא לא פליני דאסור כי פליני
אליבא דר"ש דאמר דבר שאין מתכוין מותר
אביי כרבי שמעון ורבא אמר עד כאן לא קא
א"ר שמעון אלא היכא דלא אפשר אבל

The midrash as it appears in the "Vilna *Shas*," an 1886 edition of the Babylonian Talmud. Photographed at the New York Public Library.

BABYLONIAN TALMUD

PESAḤIM 25b

A man came to Rava and said to him: The governor of my town has ordered me to kill another man. If I do not kill as he ordered, he will have me killed. What shall I do?

Rava replied: Do not kill another, even if your own life is forfeit. How do you know that your blood is redder than his? Perhaps his is redder.

IN THIS MIDRASH HALA-khah the legal question is quite clear: May I kill another human being to save my own life? Rava's answer is equally clear: You may not kill an innocent person, even if you must sacrifice your own life.

This decision seems very broad; it might even be read to mean that no killing is justified because there is no way to tell whether your "blood is redder than his." In other words, how do you know that you are worthier of life than the intended victim?

However, we must remember that Mishnah and Talmud are case law—decisions on individual cases—and are not legislation. The centuries during which Mishnah and Talmud grew included many decades of persecution and subjugation. In those years, many of the cases brought before the rabbis dealt with questions of life and death, ransom and sacri-fice. These very serious problems often required long and technical discussions. But the decisions in each case were based on specific facts presented to the rabbinical court. The rabbis were not acting as lawmakers or legal philosophers; they were deciding individual cases in which individual lives were at stake.

When Rava said, you cannot kill another merely to save your own life, his judgment was on a specific case. The case involved a man being ordered to kill another for no reason, except that if the man did not carry out the king's command, he himself would be put to death. Rava did not mean to include in his decision every possible killing in defense of life. For example, he did not mean to rule out killing someone who is intent on taking your life, a person the Talmud calls a "pursuer." The case for self-defense is handled fully, and quite differently, in other sections of the Talmud.

The Jerusalem Talmud treats a similar case a little differently:

> If a company of Israelites on a journey meets a band of heathens who say, "Deliver us up one of your number, and we will kill him; if not we will kill you all." Then they [the Israelites] may not do this [give up one of their number]. But if they [the heathens] say, "Deliver us up such a one, [mentioning him by name] and we will kill him; if not we will kill you all." Then they [the Israelites] may deliver him up. One Rabbi said: Yes, but only if the named one had committed a crime for which he is liable to be put to death. Rabbi Johanan said: Even without this restriction.

Here the law is clear: If the "heathens" say they will allow the group, the Jewish community, to go free if the Jews select one person to be offered as sacrifice, then the group must risk the chance of death. No Jewish community may choose who shall die and who shall live. "How do you know that your blood is redder than his?" However, if the "heathens" name the person who shall be killed to save the group, this person *may* be given up.

The law is clear, and yet another midrash tells us what happens when the law is applied too strictly: Ulla ben Kishev was under sentence of death by a Roman governor. Roman soldiers sought Ulla everywhere. He ran away and found refuge with Rabbi Joshua ben Levi, in the town of Lud. The Roman soldiers learned that Ulla was in Lud and encircled the town. The Roman governor offered the Jews of Lud a choice: either give up Ulla for execution, or the town and its inhabitants would be destroyed.

The law was clear: Ulla had been named specifically by the Romans, and the townspeople had the right to deliver Ulla to the executioners to save many lives. But, the Midrash continues, the Jews of Lud refused. They said they would all die rather than turn one of their teachers over to the Romans. Rabbi Joshua ben Levi went to Ulla and told him of the choice before the Jews of Lud. Joshua persuaded Ulla to give himself up to the Romans. Lud and its inhabitants were saved.

The Talmudic midrash does not end there. A story is added, as if to make the point that righteousness does not always follow from strict application of the law: Rabbi Joshua ben Levi was a very learned and pious man. So much so, says the midrash, that the prophet Elijah frequently spoke to Joshua in his dreams. But after Joshua persuaded Ulla to give himself up to the Romans, Elijah did not appear in Joshua's dreams. So it went for a long, long time. Joshua prayed and fasted, fasted and prayed until, after years, Elijah finally reappeared to him. When Joshua asked Elijah why he had not appeared to him for so long, Elijah said, "Shall I reveal myself to an informer?" Joshua defended himself, "But I only followed the law given us by the sages. And Elijah answered, "Is this a teaching that a godly person should follow?" □

STUDY QUESTIONS

1 What would your advice have been had someone asked you the same question that was asked of Rava?

2 Under what conditions does the Talmud allow one person to kill another? What moral and legal principle do the rabbis invoke to justify killing?

Do you believe there are conditions under which one may kill? What about war?

3 Can you think of any modern nation that simply refuses to defend itself against aggression (on the grounds that such defense would inevitably lead to the taking of life)? What do you think would happen to such a nation?

4 The Jerusalem Talmud seems to waver over the question of whether or not it is right to hand someone over for execution, and particularly when that someone is Jewish and his executioners are non-Jews. One rabbi takes the position that it *is* permissible to hand over that individual, but *only* if he has actually committed a capital crime. Rabbi Johanon, however, takes the position that it simply doesn't matter whether or not the accused individual has committed any crime at all.

Which of these two positions do you agree with and why? Do you believe that it is ethically and legally just to sacrifice an innocent man if his sacrifice will assure the survival of the community?

5 Had you been in Rabbi Joshua's predicament, what would you have done?

6 Should one's first and deepest loyalties be to family and friends, or to the community and its laws?

7 Why does Elijah rebuke Rabbi Joshua and call him an informer? Didn't Rabbi Joshua do exactly what at least one Talmudic ruling urges?

אל תקח מאתו נשך ותרבית וירֵאתָ מֵאֱלֹהֶיךָ וְחֵי אָחִיךָ עִמָּךְ :

עג אל תקח מאתו נשך ותרבית ממנו אי אתה לוקח אבל אתה נעשה לו ערב :

עד איזהו נשך ואיזהו תרבית . איזהו נשך המלוה סלע בה' דינרים שאתים חטים בג' מפני שהוא נושך . איזהו תרבית המרבה בפירות . ביצד לקח המנו חטים מדינר זהב גבור ובן השער עמדו חטים בשלשה דינרים . אומר לו תן לי חיטיי שאני מוכרם ולוקח אני לי בהן יין אומר לו דרי חיטין עשויות עלי בשלשה דינרים והרי לך אצלי בדם יין ויין אין לו אם יש לו חייב ליתן לו :

עה [:] וחי אחיך עמך זו דרש בן פטורי שנים שהיו הולכים במדבר ואין ביד אחד אלא קיתון של מים אם שותהו א' מגיע לישוב ואם שותים אותו שניהם שניהם מתים דרש בן פטורי ישתו שתיהם וימותו שנאמר וחי אחיך עמך . א'ל ר'ע וחי אחיך עמך חייך קודמים לחיי חברך :

אֶת כַּסְפְּךָ לֹא־תִתֵּן לוֹ בְּנֶשֶׁךְ וּבְמַרְבִּית לֹא־תִתֵּן אָכְלֶךָ :

עו כספך ולא כסף אחרים . ואכלך ולא אוכל אחרים . או כספך ולא כסף מעשר ואכלך ולא אוכלי בהמה כשהוא אומר נשך כסף לרבות כסף מעשר נשך אוכל לרבות אוכלי בהמה :

אֲנִי יְהוָֹה אֱלֹהֵיכֶם אֲשֶׁר־הוֹצֵאתִי אֶתְכֶם מֵאֶרֶץ מִצְרַיִם לָתֵת לָכֶם אֶת־אֶרֶץ כְּנַעַן לִהְיוֹת לָכֶם לֵאלֹהִים :

עז אני ה' מכאן אמרו כל המקבל עליו עול רבית מקבל עול שמים וכל הפורק ממנו עול רבית פורק ממנו עול שמים . אני ה' אלקיכם אשר הוצאתי אתכם על תנאי כך הוצאתי אותם מא'ם על תנאי שתקבלו את מצות רבית שכל המודה במצות רבית מודה ביצ'ם וכל הכופר במצות רבית ביצ'ם כאילו כופר ביצ'ם

[ד] לתת לכם את ארץ כנען להיות לכם לאלקים מכאן אמרו כל ב'י היושב בא'י מקבל עליו עול מלכות שמים וכל היוצא לח'ל כאילו עובד כו'ם וכן בדוד הוא אמר ארוהים הם בירגשוני היום מהסתפח בנחלת ה' לאמר לך עבוד אלקים אחרים . וכי עלתה ע'ד שדוד הפלך עובד כום אלא שהי' דורש ואומר כל היושב בא'י מקבל עליו

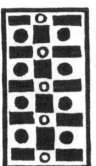

SIFRA

BEHAR SINAI 5

Rabbi Ben Petura explained the passage: "That thy brother may live with thee." [LEVITICUS 25:36]

Two men were traveling through the desert, and only one had a flask of water. The water was enough to keep only one man alive until they reached the next water hole. If the owner of the flask of water kept it for himself, he would reach the spring; if he shared it with his fellow traveler, both would die. Rabbi ben Petura said: "The verse: 'That thy brother live with thee' means that the water should be shared, even though both men die."

But Rabbi Akiva said: "'That thy brother live with thee' means that your life takes precedence over your friend's. The water should be used to save a life."

THIS MIDRASH POSES A question that modern philosophers, particularly those who try to deal with the ethics of conservation and the environment, have rediscovered. Today the problem is called the "lifeboat question": A ship goes down and a lifeboat is launched; it is capable of carrying nine people to safety. Twelve people clamber aboard the nine-passenger lifeboat. The slightest wind, any wave, will swamp the boat. Should three people be forced out of the boat to save the nine? And if so, how do you pick which people should be thrown into the water?

The environmental philosophers consider this question extremely relevant because the world population could someday exceed the world's capacity to produce food. If that happens, they ask, do we share equally what we have, so that the whole world might starve to death? Or do we allow some nations to die to keep the rest alive?

Our Sages dealt with this problem centuries before the advent of environmentalism. However, they did not pose the question in world terms. They posed it in simpler, more human terms: Two people are in a life-threatening situation. Only one can get out. Should one person escape or should both die together?

On the question of self-sacrifice and survival, two rabbis offer opposing views. Rabbi ben Petura gives the romantic answer, a kind of Romeo and Juliet answer: If we cannot live together, we shall die together.

But Rabbi Akiva, whose decisions are generally the ruling ones, gives a more rational answer, even though it is a much harsher one: We must choose life. If we cannot choose life for all, then let us choose life for those whose lives can be chosen.

And how shall we decide whose life should be saved? No one can say with absolute certainty that one life is worthier than another—that this one deserves to die less than that one. These are subjective judgments that vary from individual to individual. Rabbi Akiva says, in effect, let us leave the decision to some objective standard, to something already decided. In this case it happens to be "whose water is it?"

Today we use pretty much the same standards to decide questions almost as important as life and death. For example, who shall work and who shall lose his job. If a factory with 400 employees has to cut back to 250, the owner can make the final decision. This decision could result in a smaller, more efficient work force. It might also result in favoritism, or keeping relatives, or some kind of kickback. As a general rule, the decision is taken out of the judgment of individuals and left to the objective standard of seniority. The people who have worked the longest are the last laid off. The calendar decides.

This objective method allows for what may seem to be unfairness. A harder worker might be laid off while a lazier one is kept on. A family head with four dependents may have to go while an unmarried person stays. But what if the family head has a millionaire father, and the unmarried person supports aged parents? No person can decide absolutely who needs the job most; there are too many factors and human judgment is fallible.

Rabbi Akiva knew that when it comes to deciding who is worthier of life, no human mind or heart can choose. Perhaps one of the travelers is the father of a large and needy family, and the other a revered scholar and teacher. How to choose? Perhaps one is young with life still before him, but he isn't a very good person, and the other is an old man who has lived all his life according to the commandments. How to choose? Perhaps one man is a bachelor, and rich, but given time he might leave his money to charity which would save many lives, and the other a poor man on his way to the wedding of his only child. How to choose?

Rabbi Akiva seems to say: First, we must choose life. We must save lives—if not all lives, then those which can be saved. But since we cannot decide whose blood is redder, we cannot choose between two lives when both can be saved. We must leave such a decision to circumstances, or to God.□

STUDY QUESTIONS

1 Which of the two Rabbinic authorities, Rabbi ben Petura and Rabbi Akiva, do you agree with?

2 If you were to follow Rabbi Akiva's advice, and in the act of saving your own life deny someone else the chance to live, would you be violating the Talmud's warning against regarding one man's blood as redder than another's?

3 Does Rabbi ben Petura suggest that we are obliged to sacrifice our own lives to help another human being? Or does he urge us to refuse to make a choice between our own survival and someone else's?

Whose position is more realistic, Akiva's or ben Petura's?

4 How would you reconcile Rabbi Akiva's argument with another Torah precept, urging every Jew to love his neighbor as much as he loves himself [LEVITICUS 19:18]. Is it possible to love one's neighbor and still deny him a drop of water that might keep him alive a while longer?

Does the commandment to love one's neighbor take precedence over one's own survival?

5 Do you think that the lifeboat analogy effectively describes the situation in today's world? Or can you think of a better analogy for the problem of scarce resources?

6 The distribution of food and wealth is a continuing source of conflict in the modern world. Some nations are plagued by persistent problems of famine and overpopulation.

Is it reasonable, and consistent with the teachings of this midrash, for the wealthier nations to sacrifice some portions of their wealth to provide adequate food supplies to poorer regions? Are prosperous peoples responsible for those who are less prosperous? Up to what point?

7 What role does chance play in determining who lives and who dies in a time of crisis? Give an example and explain your answer.

ליתן אבין לראשים משופטי נפשו ·
ש"מ יש לך אדם שם לגפשו שני
שופטים : לא שנק מר חי לכל
בריה · אם אחזה מן הביטנים אין
לך לדין נחור בפולם · לרסטי
נמורי. הטולם הזה שאין להם בפולם
הבא כלום ולריכין לימול שכרן כאן
פגון אחאב שהיה עשיר מאד דקאמר
ליה בן הד כספך וזהב לי הוא
(מלכים א כ) לגדיקי נמורי לפוה"ב-
שאין להם בעוה"ז כלום כגון רבי
חגינא בן דוסא שדי לו בקב חרובין
מפרב שנה לפרב שבת("תענית כד):
לכך נאמר בכל מאדך · מן האחיב
עליך · והיה מקבל פליו טול מלכות
שמם · קורא קריאת שמע · ממחים
ידך י' ממחים · מידך היה לו למות
ולא מידי בשר ודם : מן הלוסים ·
מקום שיטולין לראוות מסם הר הבית
ומסם והלאה אין יסולין לראותו :
ובריואה · סיטל לראוות מסם פרש
אם מקום נמוך הוא · ובשאן גדר ·
מפסיק בין להר הבית : ובזמן
שהשכינה סורק · סבית אמיקש
קים: והגפנה ביהודה לא יפנה מזרח

שביק מר חי' לכל בריה ואמר רבא לא
איברי עלמא אלא לרשיע נמורי או לצדיקי
נמורי אמר רבא לידע אינש בנפשיה אם
צדיק גמור הוא אם לאו אמר רב לא איברי
עלמא אלא לאראב בן עמרי ולר' חנינא
בן דוסא לאראב בן עמרי העולם הזה ולרבי
חנינא בן דוסא העולם הבא : ואהבת את
יי אלהך : *תניא ר' אליעזר אומר אם
נאמר בכל נפשך למה נאמר בכל מאדך
ואם נאמר בכל מאדך למה נאמר בכל
נפשך אלא אם יש לך אדם שנופו חביב
עליו ממממנו לכך נאמר בכל נפשך ואם
יש לך אדם שממונו חביב עליו מגופו לכך
נאמר בכל מאדך *רבי עקיבא אומר בכל
נפשך *אפילו נוטל את נפשך **תנו רבנן**
פעם אחת נזרה מלכות הרשעה שלא יעסקו
ישראל בתורה בא פפוס בן יהודה ומצאו
לרבי עקיבא שהיה מקהיל קהלות ברבים
ועוסק בתורה אמר ליה עקיבא אי אתה
מתירא מפני מלכות אמר לו אמשול לך
משל למה הדבר דומה לשועל שהיה מהלך
על גב הנהר וראה דגים שהיו מתקבצים
ממקום למקום אמר להם מפני מה אתם
בורחים אמרו לו מפני רשתות שמביאין עלינו בני אדם אמר להם רצונכם
שתעלו ליבשה ונדור אני ואתם כשם שדרו אבותי עם אבותיכם אמרו לו אתה הוא שאומרים עליך
פקח שבחיות לא פקח אתה אלא טפש אתה ומה במקום חיותנו אנו מתיראין במקום מיתתנו על אחת
כמה וכמה אף אנחנו עכשיו שאנו יושבים ועוסקים בתורה שכתוב בה °כי הוא חייך וארך ימיך כך
אם אנו הולכים ומבטלים ממנה עאכ"ז אמרו לא היו ימים מעטים עד שתפסוהו לר"ע וחבשוהו בבת
האסורים ותפסו לפפוס בן יהודה וחבשוהו אצלו אמר לו פפוס מי הביאך לכאן אמר לו אשריך רבי
עקיבא שנתפסת על דברי תורה אוי לו לפפוס שנתפס על דברים בטלים בשעה שהוציאו את ר' עקיבא
להריגה זמן קש היה והיו סורקים את בשרו במסרקת של ברזל והיה מקבל עליו עול מלכות שמים
אמרו לו תלמידיו רבנו עד כאן אמר להם כל ימי הייתי מצטער על פסוק זה בכל נפשך אפילו נוטל
את נשמתך אמרתי מתי יבא לידי ואקיימנו ועכשו שבא לידי לא אקיימנו היה מאריך באחד עד שיצתה
נשמתו באחד יצתה ב"ק ואמרה אשריך ר"ע שיצאה נשמתך באחד אמרו מלאכי השרת לפני הקב"ה זו *תורה
וזו שכרה °ממתים ידך יי' ממתים וגו' אמר להם חלקם בחיים יצתה בת קול ואמרה אשריך ר"ע *שאתה
מזומן לחיי העוה"ב : °לא יקל אדם את ראשו כנגד שער המזרח שהוא מכוון כנגד בית קדשי הקדשים
וכו' : אמר רב יהודה אמר רב לא אמרו אלא מן הצופים ולפנים וברואה גמי א"ר אבא בריה דרבי
חייא בר אבא הכי אמר רבי יוחנן לא אמרו אלא מן הצופים ולפנים וברואה ובשאן גרי ובזמן שהשכינה
שורה תניך דגפנה ביהודה לא יפנה מזרח ומערב אלא צפן ודרום ובגליל לא יפנה אלא מזרח ומערב
ורבי יוסי מתיר שהיה ר' יוסי אומר לא אסרו אלא ברואה ובמקום שאין שם גד ובזמן שהשכינה שורה
וחכמים אוסרים חכמים היינו ת"ק איכא בניהו צדדין תניא אידך דגפנה ביהודה לא יפנה מזרח ומערב
אלא צפן ודרום ובגליל צפן ודרום מותר ורבי יוסי מתיר שהיה רבי יוסי אומר בזמן

רבי מטינא אסר בכל מקום ·
מזרח אחוריו ופניו למערב
ומסקינן אפילו כיון לארך ופרש

שאן בית המקדש קים מותר רבי עקיבא אסר בכל מקום רבי עקיבא
דינו חק איכא בניתו דון לארין רבה הו שדיין ליה לבני מזרח
ומערב אבי שרתתו צפון ודרום על רבה תרגנגדו אמר מאן דאי

שאמן כנגד ירושלים ממם לתנא
קמא לדין נמי אסרי' דהא הגפנה
ביתוסא קאמר כל יהודה מבחתו ורבנן
בתראי סברי כנגד ירושלים ממם
אסור אבל לגודדין מותר דהא אדר'
יוסי קיימי דאמר לא אסרו אלא
ברואה אבל ברחוין לא ואפילו כנגד
ירושלים ממם ואחו רבנן למימר
וחכמים אוסרים אפילו שלא ברואה
ואפילו בזמן זה ומירו עד ירושלים
לא : בדר' מקיבא נרסגין בכל מקום
סלק בחולה לארן נמי קאמר : הו
שדיין ליה לבני · לבנים שוכב עליין
לפתום היו מתורגים וקתופות טל
לדרין ראשן א' למזרח ורבצו למערב
לבנר אחת לגפון ולבנר אחת לדרום
והוא יושב על האחת ופניו בינתים
נמצא הוא נגפנת לפון ודרום ולא היה
רואה לפתח נבבל מזרח ומערב לפי
שבגבל במזרחה של ארן שצ'אל צומדת
שלא יהא פרושו לא מלפניו ולא
מלאחריו לנד לאין ישראל : חזל אבי
שדתתו לפון ודרום לראוות חם יקפיד
רבו עליך תיסבירא ליה כר'ע דאמר
בחו"ל נמי קפדין עלה דמילסא :
לתר

BABYLONIAN TALMUD

BERAKHOT 61b

In the time of Rabbi Akiva, the Roman Emperor Hadrian banned all the practices of Judaism. Anyone who dared to teach the Torah would be cruelly killed. A friend came to Rabbi Akiva to warn him that if Akiva continued to teach, he risked execution. Rabbi Akiva told his friend a story:

One day a fox passed a lake and saw the fish darting about in fear. He stopped and asked the fish why they were so scared. "Don't you see the fishermen upstream with their nets? Soon they will be here."

The fox said to the fish, "Come up here on land and I will protect you."

The fish answered, "And we thought foxes were clever. If we are in danger in the water, which is our home, how much more dangerous would it be to leave our home and go live with a fox?"

Rabbi Akiva said, "If we are in danger when we study Torah, which is our home, how much greater would be the danger if we ceased to study?

RABBI AKIVA'S STORY OF the fox and the fishes needs no further explanation, except to note that in these early midrashim the fox isn't always a bad guy. Sometimes foxes were good guys, as in the midrash about the fox and the Angel of Death (see the Introduction).

A good midrash has to have a purpose beyond entertainment. It must make a point. A chapter in Jewish history shows exactly what Rabbi Akiva was driving at when he told the story of the fox and the fish.

In the first century B.C.E., the Jews were split into two major contending parties, the Pharisees and the Sadducees. These two parties differed on political, social, and religious goals. At the heart of their division was a difference on how the Torah was to be interpreted. The Sadducees said that the Torah must be taken literally; the strict word of the Torah must be followed. The Pharisees said that the Torah should be interpreted broadly, according to the Oral Law. The division became very bitter.

After Queen Alexandra died in 69 B.C.E. her oldest son Hyrcanus, who was supported by the Pharisees, claimed the throne. The younger son Aristobulus, supported by the Sadducees, raised a civil war to take the throne for himself. After several years of civil war, the weary combatants asked Rome, the new ruler of the Mediterranean world, to choose between Sadducee and Pharisee.

The fish had asked the fox to judge between them.

Pompey, the Roman general in the East, decided that Aristobulus and the Sadducee party should have the Jewish throne. Of course, this decision was not made in the interests of the Jews but in the interests of Rome.

Now on the outside of power, the Pharisees asked Pompey to abolish the kingship so that Jews would stop fighting among themselves. Pompey was happy to do so; he sent a Roman army to take control of Jerusalem.

Aristobulus did not give up easily; he fought the Roman takeover. For three months the Sadducee army held the besieged Temple area against the Roman legions. They might have held it longer but they were defeated by their own strict interpretation of Torah. The Romans breached the Temple walls on the Sabbath when the Sadducee army would not fight. As the Romans entered the Temple area they found its Jewish defenders at prayer, unresisting. Twelve thousand Jews died as the independent state of Judah came to an end.

Having voluntarily entered the world of the foxes, the fish were eaten. □

STUDY QUESTIONS

1 In Rabbi Akiva's parable, who is the "fish" and who is the "fox"? What is the "water"?

What is the message of this midrashic fable?

2 Would it not have been more practical for Rabbi Akiva to have given up teaching and studying Torah, at least until Hadrian's ban against the practice of Judaism had been lifted?

How would Akiva have replied to that question?

3 Akiva and many of his contemporaries died a martyr's death rather than renounce their faith.

Where in this parable does Akiva make it plain that he is prepared for martyrdom?

4 Who were the Pharisees and the Sadducees? On what points of faith and politics did they disagree? You will have to consult outside research sources to answer this question.

5 On what pretext did the Romans enter Judea and annex it to their growing empire?

6 During which other periods of Jewish history have Jews been forbidden to study Torah or practice Judaism? You will probably need to do some additional research or review your previous knowledge of Jewish history to answer the question.

FOR DISCUSSION

Let us suppose that you—and not Rabbi Akiva—have just been informed that the leaders of the country in which you have lived your entire life have just declared Judaism to be illegal, and have threatened to imprison, and perhaps execute, anyone caught practicing any type of Jewish ritual.

How would you respond? Would you
1. Make a public display of your faith and thereby invite punishment (and even martyrdom)?
2. Practice Judaism secretly, while publicly disavowing it?
3. Try to flee the country?
4. Join an armed rebellion to overthrow the government?

Give historical examples for each of these responses.

ד'א פרי עץ הדר, (קמז) אלו ישראל, מה אתרוג זה יש בו ריח, ויש בו טעם,
כך ישראל יש בהן בני אדם שהם בעלי תורה, ובעלי מעשים טובים,
כפות תמרים, אלו ישראל, מה תמרה יש בה טעם, ואין בה ריח. כך ישראל
יש בהן בעלי תורה, ואין בהם מעשים טובים, וענף עץ אבות, אלו ישראל,
מה הדס זה, יש בו ריח ואין בו טעם, כך ישראל יש בהם בני אדם שיש
בידיהם מעשים טובים ואין בהם תורה. וערבי נחל, אלו ישראל, מה ערבה זו,
אין בה לא טעם ולא ריח, כך ישראל יש בהן בני אדם, שאינן בעלי תורה,
ולא מעשים טובים, אמר הקב"ה לאבדן אי אפשר, אלא יעשו כולם אגודה אחת,
(קיז) והן מכפרין אלו על אלו, לפיכך משה מזהיר את ישראל ואומר להם ולקחתם
לכם ביום הראשון.

(קיח) א'ר ברכיה בש"ר אבא בר כהנא, בזכות ולקחתם לכם ביום הראשון,
אני

הערות ותקונים.

דבר עגול עכ"ל, וטעה במח"כ, כי טרגנון הוא בעל שלש נלעות, כמאמרם נזיר ח' ע"א,
סן אחת, דינון שתים, טריגון שלש, טעריגון ארבע, לכן נ"ל בפסיקתא בטטרינון והיא
המלה היונית טעטראעעעעפ, פי' ד' זויות, ור"ל שלא היו יושבין ארבע נלעות אלא
אסטרוונגלון, ר"ל בעגול, כי המלה היונית סעעעעעעפ פירש עינול, והמלות "שורה
ארוכה" "כחצי גורן עגולה" צריך למחיק מן הספר, כי נוספו מאוח מעתיק, אחרי רואו
במשנה סנהדרין ל"ו ע"ב, סנהדרין היתה כחצי גורן עגולה, ופי' רש"י בעגולה כו' שאם
היו יושבין בשורה כו'. לכן הציב אבל בוטרגנון "שורה ארוכה", ואבל אסטרוונגילין "כחצי
גורן עגולה" ופתרון האמתי נעלם ממנו, עיין ערך מלין נד קנ"ג, (קטו) לפני סנהדרין,
אח"ז נשמטו הדברים האלה, "וערבי נחל אלו אלו סופרים הדיינן שהיו עומדין לפני סנהדרין"
אחד מימין ואחד משמאל, והשמיט המעתיק מן סנהדרין ח', עד סנהדרין ב', ונאמר
לנכון בכ"י אקספארד, וילקוט אמור, ונמורת המאור סימן ק"ג נתם הפסיקתא. וכן
יסד הפייטן שם בערבה להמשיל מחוקקי מנלה, ובו"יר אמור, אלו ג' סופרים של דיינין
שעומדים לפניהם וכותבים דברי המזכים ודברי המחייבין, וכ"ה במשנה סנהדרין שם. אבל
במשנה שבא"ם הני' לסיכך, דברי מחייבין ודברי מזכין, וכחב ע"ז הנאון מהרי"ב בהנהותיו
וח"ל נ"ל דברי המזכין ודברי המחייבין, וכך איתא במשנה שבשמנית, וכן הובא לעיל דק
ל"ד ע"א, ול"ס ע"ב, וכ"כ מפירש"י דהכא עכ"ל, וראו להוסיף עוד ראיה לדבריו שכן
הוא נו"יר פ"ל כמו שהבאתי, (קמז) אלו ישראל, מוצא במאה שערים להר"י ניאות דק
ל"ס, ועפ"ז יסד הסקליר בפיוט הכ"ל בהדר לכנות שלמים תמימים, בכפות לכנות בעלי
מעשים נעימים כו', עד עקשים אטומים מלהריח, כולו הוא עפ"י דברי הפסיקתא פה,
וכן נסמוך ליום ראשון, וכמו בעץ סדר ריח וטעס כן בעס זו בעלי מצות וידע נועס,
וכמו בכך חומר טעס ולא ריח, כן בעס זו בעלי מנות כו'. (קיז) ודן מכפרין אלו על
אלו, כ"ה נס בכ"י אקספארד, וילקוט אמור רמז תרנ"א נתם הפסיקתא, אבל בכ"י

The midrash as it appears in the 1868 edition of *Pesikta de Rab Kahana* (printed in Lyck, Poland).
Photographed under the auspices of the Jewish Theological Seminary Library.

PESIKTA DE RAB KAHANA

PISKA 27:9

In ordering the festival of Sukkot, the Torah says: "You shall take the fruit of goodly trees, boughs of palm trees, branches of thick trees, and willows of the brook ..." [LEVITICUS 23:40]

"The fruit of goodly trees" is the *etrog*, which represents certain people in Israel. Just as the etrog has a sweet smell and is good to eat, so are there people in Israel who have knowledge of Torah and do good deeds.

"Boughs of palm trees" represent certain other people in Israel. Just as the palm tree has edible fruit but no sweet aroma, so are there people in Israel who know Torah but do not do any good deeds.

"Branches of thick trees" (myrtle trees) represent another group of people in Israel. Just as the myrtle has a sweet smell but does not have edible fruit, so are there people in Israel who have no knowledge of Torah but do good deeds.

"Willows of the brook" stand for still another group of people in Israel. Just as the willow has neither a sweet smell or edible fruit, so are there people who have neither knowledge of Torah nor the merit of good deeds.

The Holy One says: In order to make it impossible for Israel to be destroyed, let all the different kinds of people be bound together into one cluster (as we do with the four kinds of plants on *Sukkot*), and the righteous among them, by their knowledge of Torah and their good deeds, will atone for all the others.

IN THE COURSE OF DIScussing the legal cases brought before them, the *Amoraim*, the Rabbis of the Talmud, often used midrashim to illustrate their decisions. Many midrashim came out of these discussions. Many more midrashim came out of the d'rashim of preachers. If that Sabbath's Torah portion was narrative or history, the darshan had a relatively easy time. Any good story teller could elaborate on the stories of Adam and eve, Noah, Abraham, Moses and Aaron. But when the portion was mainly a repetition of the laws, or gave detailed instructions for celebrating holidays, stories didn't fit. Then the great weavers of midrashim used the text as the basis for ethical and moral lessons. Rab Kahana was one of the greatest of these teachers of ethics.

The portion of the Torah called Emor [LEVITICUS 22-24] is read each year during the spring. It concerns the rules of cleanliness and celebrating holidays, and is not a very exciting portion. So Rab Kahana, using something as simple as the four species of plants carried in the synagogue celebration of Sukkot, gave a midrash which taught Jews three basic lessons:

First: a Jew is a Jew whether he is learned in Torah or not, whether he follows the Law or doesn't. Membership in the community of Israel is not determined by exams or what other people think of you.

Second: all Jews, whether scholarly or ignorant, observant or non-observant, good people or not so good, must cleave to the Jewish community, protect and help one another.

Third: Jews should not be arrogant about their knowledge or their good deeds. The willows of the brook, without either aroma or edible fruit, add as much to the combined strength of the cluster as the fruit of goodly trees.

Rab Kahana did not say that all the different kinds of Jews were equally worthy. He graded them. At the top are those who know Torah and who follow its laws. Next are those who know Torah but are not just, merciful or righteous. Third are those who have never studied, yet follow the *mitzvot*. Last are those who neither know nor do good deeds.

But, says the midrash, if we all remember that we are Jews, and help each other, then the virtues of the good will help overcome the lacks in the less good.

About 1,300 years after Rab Kahana wrote this midrash, the American patriot John Dickinson wrote a song celebrating the American Revolution. He wrote, "By uniting we stand, by dividing we fall." Dickinson was echoing Rab Kahana's advice to the Jews.□

STUDY QUESTIONS

1 The portion of the book of Leviticus from which Rab Kahana has taken his sermon is concerned with the ritual of Sukkot. How does he find in the Torah's listing of plants to be used on Sukkot a clue to an understanding of Jewish life and faith?

2 According to Rab Kahana, is it better to know a great deal about the Torah and its laws, or to practice good deeds? Do we have to choose between being learned and being good?

3 Does Rab Kahana encourage Jews who are studious and devout to separate themselves from those who are not? Does he permit any Jew to feel contempt for any other?

4 What does the image of the cluster signify to Rab Kahana?

Why is it necessary for all Jews—learned and ignorant, observant and nonobservant—to hold together, and to accept one another?

5 If you were responsible for composing a sermon for Sukkot, and you had chosen the same text Rab Kahana had before him, what lesson would you derive from the four kinds of plants used on Sukkot?

6 Does Rab Kahana's cluster, or community, leave room for individual freedom? Or must the individual always place the community's interest above his own?

FOR DISCUSSION

Some ultra-orthodox communities, both in the U.S. and in Israel, have segregated themselves from the rest of contemporary Judaism, not only by living apart from other Jews in isolated communities, but also by adopting an attitude of hostility toward Jews they consider less observant.

How do you think Rab Kahana would have reacted to this behavior?

זה הוא תנור של עכנאי מאי עכנאי אמר רב
יהודה. אמר שמואל שהקיפו דברים כעכנא
זו ומצאוהו תנא באותו היום השיב רבי
אליעזר כל תשובות שבעולם ולא קבלו
הימנו אמר להם אם הלכה כמותי חרוב זה
יוכיח נעקר חרוב ממקומ מאה אמה ואמרי
לה ארבע מאות אמה אמרו לו אין מביאין
ראיה מן החרוב חזר ואמר להם אם הלכה
כמותי אמת המים יוכיח חזרו אמת המים
לאחוריהם אמרו לו אין מביאין ראיה מאמת
המים חזר ואמר להם אם הלכה כמותי כותלי
בית המדרש יוכיחו הטו דטו כותלי
בית המדרש ליפול נער בהם רבי יהושע
אמר להם אם תלמידי חכמים מנצחים זה
את זה בהלכה אתם מה טיבכם לא נפלו
מפני כבודו של רבי יהושע ולא זקפו מפני
כבודו של ר"א ועדיין מטין ועומדין חזר
ואמר להם אם הלכה כמותי מן השמים
יוכיחו יצאתה בת קול ואמרה מה לכם אצל
ר"א שהלכה כמותו בכ"מ עמד רבי יהושע
על רגליו ואמר °לא בשמים היא מאי לא בשמים
בשמים היא אמר רבי ירמיה שכבר נתנה
תורה מהר סיני °אין אנו משגיחין בבת קול
שכבר כתבת בהר סיני בתורה °אחרי רבים
להטת אשכחיה רבי נתן לאליהו א"ל מאי
עביד קב"ה בההיא שעתא א"ל קא חייך
ואמר נצחוני בני נצחוני בני אמרו °אותו
היום הביאו כל טהרות שטיהר ר"א ושרפום
באש ונמנו עליו וברכוהו ואמרו מי ילך
ויודיעו אמר להם ר"ע אני אלך שמא ילך
אדם שאינו הגן ויודיעו ונמצא מחריב את

The midrash as it appears in the "Vilna *Shas*," an 1886 edition of the Babylonian Talmud.
Photographed at the New York Public Library.

BABYLONIAN TALMUD

BABA METZIA 59b

The Rabbis were discussing the ritual cleanliness of an oven. Everyone agreed that it was not ritually clean except for Rabbi Eliezer who kept insisting it was clean.

Rabbi Eliezer gave all manner of arguments to prove his point but the other Sages would not accept them. So Eliezer appealed to Heaven itself. "Lord," he said, "If the Law is according to my interpretation, let this carob tree prove it." And the carob tree which stood outside the house of the Sages moved a hundred cubits away.

But the Sages said, "The carob tree may move but that doesn't prove anything."

Rabbi Eliezer said, "If the Law is as I said it was, let this stream prove it." And the stream which ran by the house of the Sages reversed its direction and flowed backward.

The Sages said, "The stream may flow upward, but that doesn't prove anything."

Rabbi Eliezer said, "If I am right, let the walls of this House of Study prove it." And the walls of the House of Study began to fall inward.

Rabbi Joshua, one of the Sages, said to the walls, "If scholars are debating, what business is that to the walls of this house?" Out of great respect for Rabbi Joshua's wisdom, the walls stopped falling. But out of respect for Rabbi Eliezer's scholarship, they remained leaning inward.

Then Rabbi Eliezer said, "If the Law is according to my interpretation, let the heavens prove it."

A voice was heard from heaven and it said, "Why do you argue with Rabbi Eliezer. The Law is as he says it is."

Whereupon Rabbi Joshua stood up and quoted from Deuteronomy [30:12], "The Law is not in heaven."

Rabbi Jeremiah explained the meaning of the verse, "The Law is not in heaven": The Torah was given once and for all on Mount Sinai. From that time onward, we do not listen to voices from heaven to interpret the Law, for God had already given the Law to man in the Torah. And interpretations of the Law, as described in the Mishnah [SANHEDRIN 4:1], are made by majority decision.

Rabbi Nathan, who was present during this debate, once met Elijah the Prophet. He asked Elijah what God had been doing while the discussion was taking place. Elijah said, "God laughed and said, 'My children have defeated Me, My children have defeated Me.'"

ONE OF THE MOST PERsistent and troublesome questions in all monotheistic religions is what is called the great theodicy: How can a perfect God allow evil to exist? How can the all-powerful, just, merciful, compassionate God allow injustice and wickedness to flourish in the world that He created?

The Rabbis taught that while the world was created perfectly, human beings were given free will and have the power to choose between good and evil. The Law shows the path to goodness, but not even heaven can force man to choose the right path.

The Rabbis created many midrashim to teach this difficult message. This talmudic midrash is one of them. It deals with the right of humans to interpret God's Torah, even wrongly.

What the Rabbis were debating is not important. It happened to have been some detail of ritual cleanliness. Rabbi Eliezar's view of the law differed with the interpretation of all the other members of the court. But Eliezar persisted in his interpretation.

Rabbi Eliezar's view was legally correct. When he appealed to a tree, then a brook, then stones of the house in which they sat, each of these inanimate, natural things acted unnaturally to show that Eliezar was right. None of these mir-acles moved the rabbis. Finally Eliezar appealed to heaven itself. A voice from heaven declared that Eliezar's interpretation was right.

Then Rabbi Joshua reminded heaven that while the Law was given from heaven, it was no longer in heaven's hands. Once the Jews accepted the Torah on Sinai, the Law was in the hands of the people. And the people had the right to interpret it, rightly or wrongly.

To make the point that this was not just clever use of the Torah to win a debater's victory, the midrash goes on to show that God had been listening to the debate and was quite pleased with the outcome. Heaven had no right to interfere with the collective judgment of the sages. That judgment could very well be wrong at times, but if human beings are to be free, they must be free to make mistakes, too. If heaven kept telling humankind what to do in every instance, then God would not have created human beings, but robots.□

STUDY QUESTIONS

1 This aggadic anecdote has all of the attributes of a folktale: a conflict of wills, a display of magic, and a sense of the supernatural hovering just overhead. Yet for all its fancifulness it still conveys a serious message. What is that message?

2 Since aggada is not the same as halacha, the opinions expressed in this midrash are not legally binding. Why then was the tale incorporated into the Talmud?

3 What does the term *theodicy* mean, and what does any theodicy assume about God?

What is the great contradiction in moral logic that every theodicy is expected to solve?

4 How does this midrash serve to demonstrate the Rabbis' confidence both in their own authority and in the necessity for human freedom?

5 Why is God pleased with Rabbi Joshua's refusal to listen to the voice from heaven?

6 Does it bother you that this midrash describes God as admitting defeat at the hands of Rabbi Joshua and his colleagues?

Did the author of this tale really believe that a Rabbi has the right to reject God's judgment? Does the authority of a Rabbi supersede that of God?

7 Why is it necessary for human beings to have sufficient freedom of will to be able to make both right and wrong decisions? What would life be like if we were unable to choose freely between right and wrong?

8 Can you think of any other figure out of Jewish legend or history who argues with God?

FOR DISCUSSION

What is the method, today, for settling disputes on points of *halakhah* or on matters of Jewish belief? Do modern rabbis appeal to precedent and logic, or to supernatural signs and wonders?

Consider a current controversy—the question, "who is a Jew?" How do today's rabbis attempt to resolve it? What method would *you* use?

מלכי אומות העולם אצל בלעם הרשע וכו' יד) וכיון ששמעו מסיו הדבר מנו כלם והלכו
איש איש למקומו ולפיכך נתבעו אומות העולם כדי שלא ליתן פתחון פה להם כלפי
שכינה לומר אלו נתבענו כבר קיבלנו עלינו הרי שנתבעו ולא קבלו עליהם שנאמר ויאמר
יי' מסיני בא [וגו'] (דברים לג) ונגלה על בני עשו הרשע ואומר להם מקבלים אתם את
דתורה אמרו לו מה כתיב בה אמר להם לא תרצח אמרו זו היא ירושה שהורישנו אבינו
שנאמר על חרבך תחיה (בראשית כז) נגלה על בני עמון ומואב אמר להם מקבלים אתם את
התורה אמרו לו מה כתוב בה אמר להם לא תנאף אמרו לו כלנו מניאוף דכתיב ותהרין
שתי בנות לום מאביהם (שם יט) והיאך נקבלה נגלה על בני ישמעאל אמר להם מקבלין
אתם את התורה אמרו לו מה כתוב בה אמר להם לא תגנוב אמרו לו כז
הברכה נתברך אבינו דכתיב הוא יהיה פרא אדם [ידו בכל] (שם טז) וכתיב כי גנוב
גנבתי (שם מ) טו) וכשבא אצל ישראל מימינו אש דת למו (דברים שם) פתחו כלם סיהם
ואמרו כל אשר דבר יי' נעשה ונשמע (שמות כד) וכן הוא אומר עמד ויתודד ארץ ראה ויתר
גוים (חבקוק ג) טז) אמר רבי שמעון בן אלעזר אם בשבע מצות שנצטוו בני נח שקבלו
עליהם אינן יכולין לעמוד בהן קל וחומר למצות שבתורה משל למלך שמנה לו שני
אפטרופסין אחד ממונה על אוצר של תבן ואחד ממונה על אוצר של כסף ושל זהב זה
שהיה ממונה על התבן נחשד והיה מתרעם על שלא מנו אותו על אוצר של כסף ושל זהב
וזה שהיה ממונה על הכסף ועל הזהב אמר לו ריקה בכסף בכפית בכסף וזהב על אחת כמה
וכמה והלא דברים קל וחומר ומה בני נח בשבע מצות בלבד לא יכלו לעמוד בהם כשש
מאות ושלש עשרה מצות על אחת כמה וכמה י) (מפני) [ומפני] יה) מה לא ניתנה תורה
בארץ ישראל שלא ליתן פתחון פה לאומות העולם לומר לפי שנתנה בארצו לפיכך לא
קבלנו: דבר אחר שלא להטיל מחלוקת בין השבטים שלא יהא זה אומר בארץ נתנה וזה
אומר בארצי נתנה לפיכך ניתנה במדבר דימום פרהסיא במקום הפקר יט): כשלשה דברים
ניתנה כ) תורה במדבר ובאש ובמים מה אלו חנם לכל באי העולם אף אלו חנם לכל באי
העולם:

אשר הוצאתיך מארץ מצרים מבית עבדים עבדים למלכים היו אתה אומר עבדים
למלכים היו או אינו אלא עבדים לעבדים כשאומר ויסדך מבית עבדים [מיד פרעה מלך
מצרים] (דברים ז) עבדים למלכים היו ולא עבדים לעבדים כא): ד"א מבית העובדים עבודה זה:

פרשה ו

לא יהיה לך אלהים אחרים על פני למה נאמר אנגיה ה) לפי שנאמר אנכי יי' אלהיך משל למלך
בשר ודם שנכנס למדינה אמרו לו עבדיו גזור עליהם גזרות אמר להם כשיקבלו את מלכותי אנגזור
עליהם שאם מלכותי לא יקבלו גזרותי לא יקבלו ג) כך אמר המקום לישראל אנכי יי' אלהיך
לא יהיה לך אני הוא שקבלתם מלכותי במצרים אמרו לו כן ד) וכשם שקבלתם מלכותי
קבלו גזרותי (לא יהיה לך אלהים אחרים על פני) רבי שמעון בן יוחאי אומר הוא שנאמר
להלן אני יי' אלהיכם (ויקרא יח) שקבלתם מלכותי בסיני אמרו הן הן קבלתם מלכותי קבלו

מאור עין יז) קיעעינוהו קסוטרים לפי מהונא לעיל ריש יתרו ובילקוט המחמר בשלימות : טו) מנבנב שתי פעמים
טיסמעאלים נגבוטו מיד היסמעאלים ז"ר ודיין נג"ר סון סס"ד וטס"ח : טז) עיין לעיל ספ"א תספרי דברים פי' סוד"ג
ונרים מסכח פ"ז: י) סיין ספרי סס ג' מאכו"כ נבל המלות שנתורה: ים) וכ"ס בילקוט: יט) סיין למיל פ"ח
בד"ה רימנו במדבר: כ) תא"א הניח נ"ח סלה וכ"ה בילקום ומ"ג ונרנה במדבר פ"א ותחנחומא נ' כמי

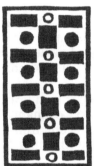

MEKHILTA

BAHODESH YITRO 5

Before Israel was offered the Torah, it was offered to the other nations, so that they would not have the excuse of saying: "Had we been asked, we would have accepted it." For behold, they were asked . . .

The Lord appeared to all the children of Esau the wicked and said to them: "Will you accept the Torah?" They said to Him: "What is written in it?" He said: "Thou shalt not murder." They said to Him: "Our father's heritage to us was to live by the sword." With that, the children of Esau refused the Torah.

God then appeared to the children of Amon and Moab. He said to them: "Will you accept the Torah?" They said to Him: "What is written in it?" He said to them: "Thou shalt not commit adultery." They said to Him: "But we are children of adulterers." So the children of Amon and Moab refused to accept the Torah.

Then God appeared to the children of Ishmael. He said to them: "Will you accept the Torah?" They said to Him: "What is written in it?" He said to them: "Thou shalt not steal." Then they said to Him: "The very blessing that was put on our father was: And he shall be as a wild ass of a man, his hand shall be upon everything." So the children of Ishmael refused the Torah.

But when God came to the Israelites and "at His right hand was a fiery law unto them, [DEUTERONOMY 33:2], they all cried out: "All that the Lord hath spoken we will do and obey."

PERHAPS THE RELIGIOUS problem most troubling to modern Jews is that represented by the phrase "Chosen People." Unfortunately, those two words have been misunderstood by the non-Jewish world as meaning that Jews consider themselves better than other people. Even more un-fortunately, some Jews have accepted that meaning.

But to a Jew, "chosen" does not mean better. It isn't that we were picked out as superior. Not at all. We voluntarily chose to carry the weight of the Law; we voluntarily chose to accept the yoke of the 613 commandments. This may make us different, as all peoples and cultures are somehow different from all others. It does not make us better.

To reinforce this principle, the Sages taught: When God resolved to create Adam, the father of all the human race, he took the dust from which He formed Adam, not from the land of Israel, the land of the Jew; not from Jerusalem, the holy city; not from Zion, the site of the Holy Temple; but He took a little earth from every corner of the earth, from east and west, from north and south. Why? So that in the future no nation could say, from my earth was Adam created; so that no people may say, we are greater, we are worthier than our neighbor, for Adam had his birth here. [SANHEDRIN 38a]

As this midrash tells it, the Torah was not handed to the Jews right away. They were not chosen to receive it. Other nations were given the right to accept it—or reject it—before the Israelites were given their chance. But each of the other nations turned it down for one reason or another. The Hebrews heard the Law and *chose* to accept it.

Of course, this midrash could also be read as showing that each of the other nations was evil in some way. The Edomites were murderers; the Moabites were adulterers; the Ishmaelites were thieves. Moreover, they refused to give up their accustomed ways. And the Israelites? Were they free of these sins? Not at all! There were murderers and adulterers and thieves among the Hebrews, too. But as a people they chose to accept a code of law which said that murder, adultery and robbery were evil. They chose a way which required them to root out such acts and to punish those guilty of these transgressions.

To reinforce this teaching, the Sages also said: The righteous of all nations (Jew and non-Jew) have a share in the world-to-come.□

STUDY QUESTIONS

1 What does the concept of the "Chosen People" imply within the context of this midrash?

2 Why does this midrash portray God as going first to other nations, and only later to Israel?

3 Why do the children of Esau, Moab, Ammon and Ishmael reject the Torah when it is offered to them? What lesson does the midrashic author communicate at this point?

4 How does this midrash try to explain the origin of the Covenant? Why is it so important that the children of Israel be portrayed as accepting the Torah willingly and obediently?

Does the Torah itself actually portray the Israelites of Moses' time as willing and obedient servants of God?

5 From the point of view of this midrash, can we say that the giving of the Torah automatically releases Jews from sin?

What distinction, if any, *does* the giving of the Torah bestow upon Israel?

6 Our midrash conceives of the giving and the receiving of the Torah as an event that was enacted once, and once only. But can't we also think of the giving of the Torah as something continuous in history—a constantly unfolding process of give and take between God and the Jews?

7 What are the implications of the Rabbis' statement that "the righteous of *all* nations have a share in the world to come"? Does this belief contradict the idea of Israel's chosenness?

FOR DISCUSSION

Consider the possible effect of this midrash on a non-Jewish reader. Would modern Jews be better off rejecting this midrash? Could it lead to a feeling of contempt for all of those "others" who rejected God's law when it was offered to them?

Or to put it another way, should we, as Jews, regard all those who reject our values and traditions as inherently bad?

השדה מה עץ הזה אם כן
מאכל יאכל ממט תאכל ואתו לא
תכרות כך תלמידי חכמים אם הגון
הוא ממט תאכל למוד הימנו ואם לא
אתו תשחית שר מעליו · בגחל
בגחל יחד · ואש יחד פני רעים
מה בגחל זה אחד מחמד את חבירו
כון סמך על גבי מבירתה · אונה
דלקת יחזוד · אין לאחד אונה דולקת
אלא ב' או ג' ביחד · יחזוד · בגלא חבר מצוה
שיחזדונו : שתהסיפין מפשות למתיב
(ג) נחלטו · אשר טולטו מתחטם
דאו תפשטגא · שחטשולין · ודכתיב טולמווניסורידעם
גבי חמולטו : ואובעיס אימם מהכא
טולא שרי טוטן וגו' והשמעו את
מלריס · וטומה הית חומל · מרה
כגון · ודכתיב פן חיים היא למחזיקים
בה כשמדליק את האור מלית את
הפליס וקוק מלה : קמיס מחודין ·
שאיולין כל שמה · התיו · משמש
להלך לו מים · וכתיב לט למיס · ילך
יאו עלמו : אם תלמיד (חכם) הגון
שמוצה ללמוד ממך מטיה לרב ולך
אלנו במחירו : ואם לא · ילך יאו
אלל הרב : ישמ מטימוקים מלה ·
אם הגון הוא אמר לו (ד) סאיר
תורה · ואם לא ישו לך לבדך ·
ואין לורים אפן : שלטה מטקיס
וללו · מים יין וחלב (ה) זו התורה ·
שלוט טוק בה כלה וידמטה ומטה ·

בכל זה עץ הזה אם פן
מאכל יאכל ממט תאכל ואתו לא
תכרות כך תלמידי חכמים אם הגון
הוא ממט תאכל למוד הימנו ואם לא
אתו תשחית שר מעליו ·

The midrash as it appears in the "Vilna *Shas*," an 1886 edition of the Babylonian Talmud.
Photographed at the New York Public Library.

BABYLONIAN TALMUD

TAANIT 7ab

The daughter of the Roman Emperor saw Rabbi Joshua ben Hananiah and remarked that so much wonderful wisdom was in such an ugly vessel.

He said to her: "Does your father, the Emperor, keep wine in earthenware jugs?"

She said to him: "In what else should he keep wine?"

He said to her: "Your family is so great and rich, you should keep your wine in vessels of gold or silver."

The princess went and told her father that earthenware jugs were not in keeping with the family position and that only vessels of gold and silver would do.

The wine was moved from jugs to precious vessels. Whereupon it turned sour. The keepers of the wine told the Emperor what had happened.

The Emperor asked his daughter: "Who told you to do this?"

She said: "Rabbi Joshua ben Hananiah."

The Emperor called Rabbi Joshua before him and said: "Why did you tell my daughter to do so?"

Rabbi Joshua said: "I answered her according to the way she spoke to me."

The Emperor asked: "Are there no handsome scholars?"

Rabbi Joshua said: "If they were ugly, they would be even more scholarly."

THIS IS AN EXAMPLE OF A fairly frequent type of midrash. First is the story, which teaches a lesson. Then comes a sort of throw-away line, a kicker, to drive the point home.

During Greek rule over Israel, roughly the last three centuries before the Common Era (B.C.E.), Greek culture almost swallowed up Jewish customs and thought. Many Jews adopted the Greek ways and Greek philosophy. Much greater importance was given to dress and adornment. Young Jews flocked to the Greek gymnasiums, took part in Greek games, cultivated their bodies instead of their minds. Outside appearance became more important than character and thoughts.

There was, of course, a reaction against the Greek ways. Wiser heads cautioned against giving up the traditional ways of living and thinking. Some Jews went to the extreme of refusing to accept anything that seemed to be Greek.

(Some modern-day Hasidim, fearful that changes in the outside world will change traditional ways, refuse change even in clothing. They insist upon wearing the same style of clothes as the founders of their sect, who lived in Eastern Europe in the eighteenth century.)

Some of the Jews of Greek and Roman times tried to teach their people a valid lesson. A beautiful face and form is not an indication of worth or virtue. A well-muscled body is not a sign of greater importance, or even of greater usefulness. An ugly face may have great wisdom behind it. A twisted form may have within it a heart full of goodness and compassion.

And, as in Rabbi Joshua's example, a common earthenware crock keeps wine much better than vessels of gold and silver.

The kicker, the last line, adds another dimension of the teaching. Undue concern about how we look to others interferes with things about which we should really be concerned. If we didn't spend so much time worrying about how we look on the outside, we might be better people on the inside.□

STUDY QUESTIONS

1 Why does Rabbi Joshua ben Hananiah tell the Emperor's daughter to place her wine in vessels of silver and gold?

2 When the Emperor asks Rabbi Joshua whether or not there are "handsome scholars," Rabbi Joshua replies that were those scholars uglier, they would be more scholarly. What is Rabbi Joshua hinting at? Does he believe that ugliness and wisdom are synonymous?

3 Can you think of anything that is externally attractive but ugly or worthless on the inside? Should we apply this same observation to human beings?

4 Do you think that most people in our society are inclined to think more about appearances—like the Emperor's daughter? Give examples to support that view.

FOR DISCUSSION

Certain aspects of modern society draw Jews away from Judaism as powerfully as Hellenistic culture drew Jews towards paganism in the time of the Maccabees. Ultimately the Maccabees rebelled against Greek rule, and against the tyranny and secularism it stood for, but what are contemporary Jews, living in democratic societies, to do? Should we withdraw into cultural ghettos, having little or nothing to do with the political and intellectual life of non-Jewish society? Or should we find other, less radical ways of reaffirming our commitment to Jewish values?

זרעך היוצא השדה (שם), (פא) אם זכיתם סוף שאתם יוצאין לזרוע בשדה, ואם
לאו סוף שהיוצא השדה מתגרה בכם, ואיזה זה עשו הרשע, דכתיב ביה איש
יורע ציד איש שדה (בראשית כ"ה כ"ז), ד"א תבואת זרעך היוצא השדה, אם
זכית סופך למיפק לחקלך, (פב) וחמי עלמא צריך מטר, ומתפלל ונענה, ואם לאו
סוף ששונאי ישראל יוצאין לקבר את בניהם השדה, שנה שנה (דברים י"ד כ"ב),
(פג) אין מעשרין משנה לחברתה, דברי ר' עקיבא, (פב) ואכלת לפני ה' אלהיך
וגו' מעשר דגנך תירושך (שם שם), אם זכית דגנך, ואם לאו דגני, כד"א ולקחתי
דגני בעתו (הושע ב' י"א), ואם זכיתם תירושך, ואם לאו תירושי, כד"א ותירושי
במועדו (הושע שם), ארשב"ל אמר הקב"ה אני אמרתי שתהיו מוציאין מעשרותיכם
(פה) מן המובחר, כיצד בא בן לוי אצלך, אם נתת לו מן המובחר, יפתח ה' לך
את אוצרו הטוב וגו' (דברים כ"ח י"ב), ואם נתת לו מן (פו) החפוריות, ומן
הקטניות, אף אני יש לי ליתן לך מן החפוריות ומן הקטניות, יתן ה' את מטר
ארצך אבק ועפר וגו' (שם שם כ"ד) ובא הלוי כי אין לו חלק ונחלה עמך וגו',
(דברים י"ד כ"ט) א"ר לולינוס דרומיה בש"ר יורה בר סימן, (פז) **אמר אתה יש**
לך ארבעה בני בתים, בנך, ובתך, ועבדך, ואמתך, ואף אני יש לי ארבעה, הלוי
והגר והיתום והאלמנה, וכולם בפסוק אחד (פח) ושמחת בחגך אתה ובנך ובתך
ועבדך ואמתך והלוי והגר והיתום והאלמנה אשר בשעריך (דברים ט"ז י"ד) אמר
הקב"ה אני אמרתי שתהא משמח את שלך ואת שלי, בימים טובים אשר נתתי
לך, אם עשית כך, אף אני משמח את שלך ואת שלי, אלו ואלו אני עתיד לשמח בבית
הבחירה, שנ' והביאותים אל הר קדשי ושמחתים בבית תפילתי וגו' (ישעיה נ"ו ז') :

חסלת פסקא עשר העשר.

הערות ותקונים.

ובתנקומא שם הסרים המלות האלה, "את כל, א"ר אב"כ רמז לפרנמטוטין", ועין תענית
דף ט' ע"א, בתום' שם ד"ה עשר, מה שהביאו בשם הספרי. (פא) לס זכיתם סוף שאתם
יוצאין, בתום' תענית שם הביאו את הדרשה הזאת בשם ר' נתן האופניאל, וזה פלא,
וכן התעורר הגאון הרי"ב שם בסנסותיו. (פב) וחמי עלמא, בתנקומא נפרדה המלה ונסייתה
לשתי מלות "על מה" גם טעות שם ויתהלל, במקום ויתפלל. (פג) אין מעשרין משנה
לחברתה, עיין ספרי פ' ראה פסקא עשר תעשר, ועיין רי"ב ע"ג. ובמשנה תרומות
פ"א ע"ס. (פד) ואכלת לפני ה', מוצא בילקוט ראה רמז תתנ"ז בשם הפסיקתא. (פה) מן
המובחר, פה חסר, ונאמר לנכון בכ"י אקספארד וכרמולי ובילקוט שם, "אף אני יש לי
ליתן מן המובחר" ודלג המעתיק מן המובחר א', עד המובחר ב'. (פו) החפוריות, בכ"י
כרמולי המעריות, וט"ס סוא, והנאמר הזה מוצא ביארוך ערך חפר א', ח"ל נסוף פסיקתא
דעשר תעשר אם נתת לי מן החפוריות כו', ופי' הולה חזה ושחת. (פז) אמר אתה יש
לך, נ"ל אמר הקב"ה לישראל אתה יש לך, וכ"ה לנכון בכ"י אקספארד וכרמולי, ובתמורת

The midrash as it appears in an 1868 edition of *Pesikta de Rab Kahana* (printed in Lyck, Poland).
Photographed under the auspices of the Jewish Theological Seminary Library.

PESIKTA DE RAB KAHANA

PISKA 10:10

The Holy One said: You have four persons in your household, and I, too, have four persons in My household. You have your son, your daughter, your manservant, and your maidservant. The four persons in My household are the Levite, the stranger, the fatherless and the widow.

Scripture speaks of all these persons, yours and Mine, in one verse: "And thou shalt rejoice in thy feast, thou, and thy son, and thy daughter, and thy maidservant, and thy manservant, and the Levite and the stranger, and the fatherless and the widow." [DEUTERONOMY 16:14]

By these words the Holy One meant: You are to bring joy to the persons in My household as well as those in your household on all the feast days that I have given you. All, those in My household and those in your household, will share in the joy of the Temple in Jerusalem. As it is written: "Even them will I bring to My holy mountain, and make them joyful in My house of prayer." [ISAIAH 56:7]

THROUGHOUT SCRIPTURE, from the first commandments to the last prophet, Jews are entreated, commanded, and warned, to care for the poor, the fatherless, the widow, and the stranger.

The commandments included the rule of *peah* by which the corners of the fields had to be left unharvested so that the poor could take what was left.

The Book of Proverbs teaches: "He who oppresses a poor man insults his Maker; he who is kind to the needy honors Him." [PROVERBS 14:31]

Amos thundered destruction on those that "trample the head of the poor into the dust of the earth, and turn aside the way of the afflicted." [AMOS 2:6]

Isaiah called the Jews to "Seek justice, undo oppression, defend the fatherless, plead for the widow." [ISAIAH 1:17]

Jeremiah tells the Jews that the Temple will be destroyed because "they judge not with justice the cause of the fatherless ... they do not defend the rights of the needy". [JEREMIAH 5:28]

And Malachi warned them that God's judgment will fall "against those that oppress the hireling in his wages, the widow and the fatherless, and that turn aside the stranger from his right." [MALACHI 3:5]

However, despite the Torah, despite the great passion of the prophets and the terrible lessons of history, the Jews, like all people, were weak. Often they forgot the warnings and messages of the Prophets. So they were constantly reminded that not only goodness of heart requires Jews to feed the hungry and shelter the homeless, but an absolute, unwavering, inescapable law of God. It is a law that must be followed by all.

So the Rabbis, like the prophets, had to keep reminding the Jews of their obligations to the poor, to the orphaned, and to outsiders.

This midrash is one such reminder. Here the lesson is that you have an obligation to care for God's family as well as your own. God's family, made up of the Temple servants, the strangers, the orphans, and the widows, includes all those who are in need.

Why are the Levites, the Temple servants, included among those who require charity from the community? When the Children of Israel came to the land of Israel, it was divided among the Twelve Tribes, each tribe getting its own area. "Only unto the tribe of Levi he gave no inheritance; the offerings of the Lord, the God of Israel, made by fire are his inheritance." [JOSHUA 13:14] The children of Levi were to be cared for by offerings from the people.□

STUDY QUESTIONS

1 In Rab Kahana's midrash, what is meant by God's "household"? Is anyone really excluded from it?

2 What is the real effect of comparing God's feelings and values with our own? Does Rab Kahana succeed in making God seem more human, or mankind more like God?

3 Why would the Levites need to receive charity of any kind? What was their function in Biblical times?

4 In what spirit does this midrash urge us to give charity to those in need? Are we permitted to give grudgingly, or to express contempt for the poor?

5 Is anyone exempt from giving charity? Are we allowed to give charity only when we want to, or are we expected to help others regularly, and out of a sense of personal and communal obligation?

And what about the poor themselves? Are they too expected to give something of themselves to others?

6 How did the prophets feel about the importance of giving charity and doing justice? How was their judgment of the people of Israel affected by their condemnation of social injustice?

7 Why does the Book of Proverbs liken a person who oppresses the poor to a person who insults God? Does God care how the rich behave towards the poor?

8 In a society where welfare agencies exist to help the poor, what kind of responsibility should individuals feel towards anyone less fortunate than themselves? Isn't it the government's responsibility to provide for them?

FOR DISCUSSION

If you were assigned the task of carrying out, as a matter of public policy, all of Rab Kahana's recommendations, how would you do it? How would you, as welfare commissioner, insure that the stranger, the orphan, and the widow were properly being cared for?

What changes, if any, would you bring about in our present policies towards the poor and the homeless?

א"ל למה את אמרת ווי · א"ל לא אמרית ווי אלא זה אמרית שכל זמן
שהאוצרות יקרין קיטין לא יהבין נרתיהון למעבד קרבא · בין חיילדא
נטלט רבי יוחנן · וקרין עליה ויתרון דעת החכמה תחיה בעליה ·
(ג· ומעשה בר' יוחנן שאהו בולטום והלך לאיסוגים · ויסב לו למזרחד
של תאנה ונתרפא · אמרין ליה הדא מנא לך · אמר לון בן דיד דכתיב
(שיאל מ' ל) ויתנו לו פלח דבלה · וקרין עליה ויתרון דעת החכמה תחיה
בעליה · ר' יסר בר יאסן הוה אתי בארפא ואתי מן טרסים ואמר ליה
טליא אנא צריך לטיבח · אמר ליה לא תיהות ליבא דיסא סבנתא ·
א"ל בעי אנא לפירקי ק"ש · א"ל קרי · א"ל בעי אנא לביכל א"ל אכול ·
כיון דאתהן ליכן · א ל אמר אתה עד שתתבול · וקרא עליה ויתרון
דעת החכמה ההוה בעליה · ר' מאיר הוה מתבעי לכלכותא וערק עבד
על הנותא דארטין · ואיצבה יהרהון יתיבין אכלון מן ההוא סינא · חמון
יתיה אמרין הוא הוא · לית הוא הוא · אמרין אם הוא הוא · אנן כרזין
ליה אין אתי אכיל עכן והוה צבע הדא אצבעותיה בדסה דחזיר · ויהב
אצבעותיה אוחרי בפומיה · טמש הא וטמש הא · אמרין דין לדין אילו
הוה ר' מאיר לא הוה עביד כן · שבקוניה וערק · וקרא עליה ויתרון דעת
ההכמה תהוה בעליה · ר' הוה רמיך בציפורין ואמרין ציפוראי כל דאתא
ואמר דמך ר' אנן קטלין ליה · אזל בר קפרא ועלל בכוותא ואדיק ליה ·
ורישיה מיכרך · ומניה בויען אמר אהיני בני ידעיה שמעוני שמעוני ·
אראלים וסצוקים אחוז ידן בלוחות הברית · נברה ידן של אראלים וחטפ
את הלוחות · אמרין ליה דמך רבי · ואמר להו אתון אמריתון אנא לא
אמינא · ולמה לא אמר דכתיב (מל'י') ומוציא דבה הוא בכ"ל קרעי
מניהון עד דאזל קליה דקריעה עד נופתחא מהלך שלשה מילין וקרא
עליה ויתרון דעת ההכמה תהוה בעליה · ר' נחמיה בשם ר' מנא מעשה
נסים נעשו באותו היום · ע"ש היה · ואיתכנשין כל קרייתא להספידא
דרבי · אשרונ'ה בתמני עשר כנישתא ואובלוניה לבית שערים ותלא לון
יומא עד רמטא כל חד וחד מישראל לביתו ומדליק לו את הנר · וצולה ל
רן וסמלא לו הבית טים · עד שעשה האהרון שבהן שקעה ההמה וקרא
הגבר שרון מצוקין אמרין ווי דהללין שבתא · יצתה בת קול ואמרה כל
מי שלא נתעצל בהספדו של רבי מזומן להיי העולם הבא בר מן קצרה
דהוה חתן ולא אתא · כיון דשמע בן סלק ומלק נרמיה מן איגרא
ונמל ומת · יצתה (ד) בת קול ואמרה אף לאגרא קצרא מזומן
להיי העולם הבא :

א [יט] ראה את מעשה האלהים כי מי יוכל לתקן את אשר עותו ·
בשעה שברא הקב"ה את אדם הראשון נטלו וההזירו על
כל אילני גן עדן ואמר לו ראה מעשי כמה נאים ומשובחין הן וכל מה
שבראתי בשבילך בראתי · תן דעתך שלא תקלקל ותחריב את עולמי ·
שאם קלקלת אין מי שיתקן אהריך · ולא עוד שאת גורם מיתה לאותו
צדיק · מ'של מ'שה רבינו לכה'ר · ה' לאשה עוברה שהיתה הבושה בבית
האסורים · ילדה שם בן גדלה שם ומתה שם · לימים עבר המלך על
פתה האסורים כשהמלך עובר התהיל אותו הבן צווח · ואומר אדני המלך
כאן גולדתי כאן גדלתי באיזה הטא אני נתון כאן איני יודע · אמר לו

וזר לרואי השמש · ד"א
שזכות אבותיו עומדת
בד ועשה והיתה
ל ארור אשר לא יקים
ר ולא עשה ולא היתה
אשר יקים כי כל ארור
עשות צל ורופה לבעלי
ה מצל הכסף · ב עלט
וטי שמעון בן שטה ·
מצא להם פתה · בלק
ין סלקין בעיין למיקרבא
דידך · ואגא פלגא מן
וקרבון · אתון אמרין
רין לינאי מלכא ההוי
עון בן שטה לא יהב
שטה ושמע שמעון בן
מן בלכותא דפרכ הוון
מרין לינאי טרי כלכא
מילי דאוריתא · אמר
א"ל הב לי מילא ושלה
ין דאתא יתיב ליה מן
ת כעים עלי · וצרת לי
דכתיב (ישיב כ"ו) הבי
א"ל ח"ו לא אפלית בך ·
על החכמה בצל הכסף·
ה דהכן כתיב בסיפריה
· אמר ליה חמית בן
לא אוריתי היא מוקרא
ה כסא דיבריך · אמר
את כדון את בקשיותך
לי למימר ברוך שאכלנו
כל אמר שאכלנו משלו
ח · ר' אבין אמר על
ן שיטתיה דר' ירטיה
בא ליה כרשב"נ והבא
אע"פ שלא אכל עמדן
והא בשם ר' איסי אמר
תני שנים שאכלו דגן
שב"ג · י ג' בלוטמין היו
ן כלבא שבוע וכל הד
והיה שם בן בטיח בן
אוצרות ראש קכרין

The midrash as it appears in a late nineteenth century *Midrash Rabbah* (printed in Vilna).
Photographed at the New York Public Library.

MIDRASH RABBAH

ECCLESIASTES 7:13

When God created the first man, He led him round all the trees in the Garden of Eden.

God said to him, "See My works, how beautiful and praiseworthy they are. Everything I have created has been created for your sake. Think of this, and do not corrupt or destroy My world; for if you corrupt it, there will be no one to set it right after you."

THIS MIDRASH COULD HAVE been written by an environmentalist in the twentieth century. It was written by a rabbi about 1,500 years ago.

The story of the creation ends with the creation of man: "male and female created He them. And God blessed them; and God said unto them: 'Be fruitful, and multiply, and replenish the earth, and subdue it; and have dominion over the fish of the sea, and over the fowl of the air, and over every living thing ...'" [GENESIS 1:28]

But the 24th Psalm begins: "The earth is the Lord's, and the fullness thereof ..."

And Isaiah warns: "He is God; that formed the earth and made it, He established it, He created it not a waste, He formed it to be inhabited." [ISAIAH 45:18]

There are similar opposing views throughout Jewish sacred literature. On one hand there is the idea that God gave man dominion (command over) all the earth and the things in it; and on the other hand, there is the idea that man is merely the caretaker of the earth and all things upon it.

The problem is with that word in Genesis: "subdue." What does it mean in the context of the Book of Genesis? For one thing, it seems to be a rather tough, warlike word to be stuck in the middle of a very poetic telling of the beginning of life. "Subdue" doesn't fit among "fruitful" and "replenish."

Maimonides explained that "and subdue it" means that humankind is allowed to plant, uproot, build, mine the earth and the like. In effect, humankind may harness the forces of nature in constructive and civilizing ways which will make it easier, even more pleasant, to be fruitful.

But our Sages remind us not to forget the "replenish" part. You may cut down a tree to build a house, but don't forget to plant another to replenish the earth. You may take fish from the sea to eat, but don't take so many that the fish will be unable to replenish themselves.

The world was given to you to enjoy, not to destroy.

On the other hand, the Rabbis also worried about those who would deny themselves things and pleasures that were permitted. The Sages didn't hold with fasting for the sake of fasting, with celibacy, with asceticism in general. (Ascetics are people who deny themselves material satisfactions and the ordinary pleasures of life.) The Rabbis held that to deny the gifts God has given us is to insult God.

"Rabbi Isaac said: Aren't the things prohibited in the Law enough for you [he meant the things denied by the laws of Kashrut and cleanliness] that you want to prohibit yourself from other

things? A vow of abstinence is like an iron collar, such as is worn around the neck by prisoners. One who imposes on himself such a vow [of abstinence] is like a man who meets a detachment of soldiers carrying such a neck-collar and voluntarily puts his head into it. Or he is like a man who drives a sword into his own body."
[TALMUD: NEDARIM 41b]□

STUDY QUESTIONS

1 Why does the author of this midrash go back to the story of the Garden of Eden just to make a point about the environment? Couldn't he have told us, simply, not to destroy our planet by polluting its atmosphere and its streams? What does he gain by beginning his sermon with the first human?

2 What does it mean to say that God has given man "dominion" over all the earth? Does that statement imply that mankind is free to do whatever it pleases?

3 When Psalm 24 declares that "the earth is the Lord's and the fullness thereof," is it really saying that nothing on earth ultimately belongs to man?

4 What significance can we attach to the fact that in the first chapter of Genesis man and woman are created last, *after* the world they are to inhabit has been brought to a state of completion?

5 How literally are we to interpret the Torah commandment to "be fruitful and multiply"? Does that mean, for example, that every married couple is obliged to have as many children as they are physically capable of producing?

6 Can you think of any way in which the commandment to take dominion over the earth might conflict with the commandment to replenish it? Is it possible or impossible to do both at once?

7 Identify at least one legitimate form of asceticism in Jewish life.

8 How did the Rabbis generally react to those who felt that God could only be served through acts of self-denial, such as fasting and celibacy? Did they encourage such behavior?

FOR DISCUSSION

How far should any society be prepared to go in order to "subdue" the earth? Are we entitled, as one species among many, to exterminate other species in our quest for survival? To what extent is it practicable for us to exploit the finite natural resources of this planet?

The midrash as it appears in the Jerusalem Talmud (1867 edition printed in Zhitomir, Ukraine). Photographed at the New York Public Library.

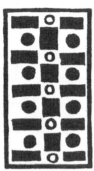

JERUSALEM TALMUD

KIDDUSHIN 1:7

A man may feed his father fattened chickens and inherit Gehenna (Hell), and another may put his father to work treading a mill and inherit the Garden of Eden.

How is it possible for a man to feed his father fattened chickens and still inherit Gehenna?

There was a man who used to feed his father fattened chickens. Once his father said to him, "My son, where did you get these?" He answered, "Old man, old man, shut up and eat, just as dogs shut up when they eat." Such a man feeds his father on fattened chickens but inherits Gehenna.

How is it possible for a man to put his father to work in a mill and still inherit the Garden of Eden?

There was a man who worked in a mill. The king ordered that millers be brought to work for him. Said the man to his father, "Father, you stay here and work in the mill in my place, and I will go to work for the king. For if insults come to the workers, I prefer that they fall on me and not on you. Should blows come, let them beat me and not you." Such a man puts his father to work in a mill yet inherits the Garden of Eden.

JEWS DO NOT BELIEVE that there is any sin in riches, nor is there any particular virtue in poverty. On the other hand, there is no special virtue in having money; nor is there any unworthiness in having none.

What is important is how you come by what you have, what you do with what you have, and how you deal with the people around you—most particularly how you treat those poorer, weaker, older than yourself.

In the first example, a man feeds his father very well. It is assumed that he also gives his father a good house to live in and good clothes. Apparently the man is rich, if he can feed his father fatted chickens. (There's a hint here that perhaps he isn't quite honest, since his father asks where he got the chickens.)

But despite the high level on which this man supports his parent, he does not find favor in heaven. The reason: he treats his father like a dog. "Eat and shut up," he says to the parent who cared for him. He denies to another human being the dignity necessary for the enjoyment of life.

In the second example is a man who truly finds favor in heaven. He takes upon himself the insults and blows that might fall upon his father. (In ancient days, and through feudal times, the king or lord collected taxes in money from those who had money and in work from those who had no money. The latter owed so many days each month of work on the roads or in the lord's fields or in the castle.)□

STUDY QUESTIONS

1 The two sons in this midrash represent two opposing patterns of behavior, one moral, the other immoral. But which one is which?

What is it that distinguishes the behavior of the good son from that of the bad son?

2 What does it mean to "inherit Gehenna"? What was Gehenna and where was it located?

Is it necessary to believe in Gehenna in order to behave respectfully towards one's parents?

3 In the Torah we are commanded by God to honor our parents, but what form should the honoring of our parents take? Are we, for example, responsible for supporting them when they are too old to work or to support themselves?

Or is it enough if we just behave politely towards them?

4 Does this midrash place any particular importance on having a lot of money? Do Jews believe that there is virtue in being either wealthy or poor?

5 If you were a parent, how would you want your children to treat you? Would you expect them to sacrifice their wealth or happiness to insure your comfort?

6 In the U.S., and in many other countries, older people are cared for through a variety of social welfare programs (like Social Security and Medicare). Does the fact that such programs exist relieve sons and daughters of their responsibility to care for their elderly parents?

7 Have you ever spoken to your parents in the same tone of voice used by the bad son when speaking to his father?

How did it make them feel? How did you feel about it afterwards?

FOR DISCUSSION

One of the problems older people face in our society is the loss of dignity that sometimes comes with aging. This is particularly true of older people who have retired from work, and whose children are themselves adults with families of their own. In such circumstances, older people may start to feel useless or irrelevant, or even worse, a burden to their children and grandchildren.

Are there ways to avoid this predicament? How can we help older people to feel useful and wanted?

כן בשעה שדביא לו ערב שלישי אמר תרע כי מפני זה אני מלוה לך •
שעמדו ישראל לקבל התורה אמר להם אני נותן לכם תורתי הביאו לי
ערבים טובים שתשמרוה ואתננה לכם • אמרו אבותינו עורבים **אותנו** •
אמר להם הקב"ה אבותיכם יש לי עליהם • ג אברהם יש לי עליו שאמר
(בראשית סו) במה אדע • יצחק יש לי עליו שהיה אוהב לעשו ו ני שנאתיו
שנאמר (מלאכי א) ואת עשו שנאתי • ד יעקב שאמר (ישעיה מ) נסתרה דרכי
מה' • אלא הביאו לי ערבים טובים ואני נותנה לכם • אמרו לפניו רבש"ע
נביאינו ערבין לנו • אמר להם יש לי עליהם שנאמר (ירמיה נ) והרועים
פשעו בי וגו' • וכתיב (יחזקאל יג) כשועלים בחרבות נביאיך ישראל היו •
אלא הביאו לי ערבים טובים ואתננה לכם • אמרו הרי בנינו עורבים
אותנו • אמר הקב"ה הא ודאי ערבים טובים על ידיהם אתננה לכם •
הה"ד (תהלים ח) מפי עוללים ויונקים יסדת עוז • ואין עוז אלא תורה •
שנאמר (שם כט) ה' עוז לעמו יתן • בשעה שהלוה נתבע ואין לו לשלם מי
נתפש לא הערב • הוי מה שנאמר (הושע ד) ותשכח תורת אלהיך אשכח
בניך גם אני • א"ר אחא גם אני כביכול אם אני בשכחתה מי יאמר בתורה
לפני ברכו את ה' המבורך לא היונקים • הוי סרפיון התורה שבבם נתפשו
בניכם שנאמר (ירמיה נ) לשוא הכיתי את בניכם • כביכול גם אני בשכחה •
מי יאמר ברכו את ה' המבורך לפני • לפיכך צריך אדם להרגיב בנו לתורה
ולהנגו בלימוד שיאריך ימים בעולם • שנאמר (משלי ם) כי בי ירבו ימיך :
ב ר' יוחנן ור' יהושע בן לוי ורבנן • ר' יוחנן אמר (א) ממה שהבנסתגו
לארץ טובה ורחבה אריך נרוצה לארעא מבתא דאתקריאת משכנותא •
ורבי"ל אמר מטה שנתת לנו ארעא מבתא רבתא דאיתקריאת משכנותא
אריך נרוצה • ורבנן אטרין מטה שהסרים שכינתך בתוכנו
כדבתיב (שמות כה) ועשו לי מקדש אריך נרוצה • ורבנן אמרין חורי •
על שטלקת שביבתך מתובנו אהרין נרוצה • תדע לך שהוא בן • שכל
צרות שבאו עליהן במעשה העגל לא נתאבלו • כיון שאמר להם משה
(שמות לג) כי לא אעלה בקרבך • מיד וישמע העם את הדבר הרע הזה
ויתאבלו • יתגו ר"ש בן יוחאי זין שנתן להם לישראל בחורב• ושם המפורש

בן עלמות אהבוך • על
א על כן עלמות אהבו...
אלו בעלי תשובה • ד"א
(עמוס יו) והבאתי את
בן עלמות אהבוך • אלו
ה' פעלך בקרב שנים
חסד שנא' (תהלים חל) כי
א על כן עלמות אהבוך •
ם ומשמרו את השבועה
מדם מתן שבתן של
ה לעשות ראש חולה
לבכם לחולה • לחולה
מצעם • והם חלים לפניו
שם) כי זה אלהים אלהינו
הגנו בעולם הזה ובעולם
ות • דבר אחר עלמות •
תופפות • ד"א עלמות
מזין אלו לאלו באוצבע •
וגהגנו עלמות • בשני
הזה דכתיב (דניאל סו) כי
ש כח) ונהך ה' תמיד •
שעה שעמדו ישראל לפני
הם הקב"ה אליעק אני
טובים שתשמרוה ואני
לנו • אמר להם אבותיכם
ללות מן המלך אמר לו
ערב אהד אמר לו ערבך •
ערבך צריך ערב • כיון

נוכב ד' • ויק"ת רבכ סוף פרשה יא"א • לקטן ים פרשה ו'• מדרש תהלים סוף מזמור פח • קהלת רבה פרבה א"י • ילקוט ישעיה רמז רע"ד •

חידושי הרמ"ש

שם כ' לנאמות תפקד כו' וכקול גדול • (א) ממס שהכנסתנו לאיץ טונב ולמצם • טראא דסטווכ פ' ארן ס תין ובוג :

פירוש מהרז"ו

וינלגו את מגרים ותרגומו ורוקינו ית מלחאי והא שמן מוזק שקק על כן עלמות אהבוך
אלו ישראל לו כמ"ש קדמו שדי• וגו' • כתוך עלמות שיפמפות וכו"ל על שאר הביאות :
יום המות • וזהו עלמות עלס מות שעלעלים מתב תמות אין טו מות וזהו עלמות דבר ומזומה

MIDRASH RABBAH

SONG OF SONGS 1:4

When the people of Israel stood at Mount Sinai ready to receive the Torah, God said to them, "Bring Me good sureties to guarantee that you will keep it, and then I will give the Torah to you."

They said, "Our ancestors will be our sureties."

God said to them, "I have faults to find with your ancestors. But bring Me good sureties and I will give it to you."

They said, "King of the Universe, our prophets will be our sureties."

He replied, "I have faults to find with your prophets. Still, bring Me good sureties and I will give the Torah to you."

They said to Him, "Our children will be our sureties."

And God replied, "Indeed, these are good sureties. For their sake I will give you the Torah."

Hence it is written: "Out of the mouth of babes and sucklings You have founded strength." [PSALMS 8:3]

JEWS HONOR THE OLD, BUT they place their faith in their children.

For every midrash about honoring the old, there is a story about the importance of children to Israel.

There is a commandment that says: "Thou shalt rise up before the hoary head." [LEVITICUS 19:32] Then there is the midrash about Israel's captivity in Babylon:

"Rabbi Judah said: 'See how beloved the little children are before God. When the Sanhedrin went into captivity, the *Shechinah* (the spirit of God) did not go with them. When the priests and Levites went into captivity, the Shechinah did not go with them. But when the children went into captivity, the Shechinah went with them.'" [LAMENTATIONS RABBAH 1:5]

If we have to choose between what has gone before and what is yet unfolding, we must choose the latter. This midrash explains why. Our ancestors had their chance and failed. Even our prophets failed. If there is hope—and God promises hope—then it is in our children.

The command to "Choose life!" may also be read "Choose the future." Our children are our future.□

STUDY QUESTIONS

1 This midrash, one of many written about the giving of the Torah to Israel, emphasizes the role of children. What, precisely, does this midrash tell us?

2 Is there any logical contradiction in a religious culture—like Judaism—that teaches both reverence for the aged and faith in the young? Is it possible to express both at once?

3 Why should God require sureties before granting Israel the Torah? Does this midrash speak of the Covenant as if it were a commercial transaction?

4 Can you see a link between faith in a generation yet to be born—which this midrash expresses—and faith in the Messiah? What connection exists between these two articles of faith?

5 Many midrashim connect the exile of Israel to the exile of God's spirit (the *Shechinah*). In Rabbi Judah's midrash, however, it is the exile of the children of Israel that causes the Shechinah to depart this world. Why is this midrash so specific about the cause of the Shechinah's departure? Why should the exile of the children of Israel matter that much?

6 Rabbi Judah's midrash offers us no account of how the Shechinah might be returned to the world. If you had to give this midrash a happy ending, how would you rewrite it? What role would the children of Israel play in reintroducing the Shechinah to the world?

7 Practically all of the major and minor festivals in the Jewish calendar are commemorative—they look backward—to some momentous event in the past.

How does this midrash look upon history, and how does its reverence of children affect its outlook?

FOR DISCUSSION

One of the common literary conventions that governs the writing of midrashim is the practice of humanizing God. In this midrash, for example, God appears as a kind of broker, dealing with a client whose collateral is not really all that good, and demanding additional security before approving a loan.

However amusing as this characterization of God may seem, it is not a particularly exalted picture of the Lord of the Universe. Some people might even think that it is degrading: that it drags God down to our level, rather than lifting us up to His. Do you agree with this criticism? How would the midrashist have answered it?

Printed in the USA
CPSIA information can be obtained
at www.ICGtesting.com
JSHW060048150824
68134JS00031B/2672